/ / / / /

BALSAMROOT
a memoir

/ / / / /

Mary Clearman Blew

UNIVERSITY OF OKLAHOMA PRESS
NORMAN

A portion of Chapter Eight first appeared in *CutBank*.

LIBRARY OF CONGRESS CATALOGING IN PUBLICATION DATA

Blew, Mary Clearman, 1939–

Balsamroot : a memoir / Mary Clearman Blew.

p.   cm.

ISBN 0-8061-3322-8

1. Port Angeles Region (Wash.)—Social life and customs.   2. Port
Angeles Region (Wash.)—Biography.   3. Clearman family.   4. Blew,
Mary Clearman, 1939–   —Family.   5. Authors, American—20th
century—Family relationships.   I. Title.

F899.P8B57   1994

979.7'99—dc20   93-34888

The paper in this book meets the guidelines for permanence and durability of the Committee on Production Guidelines for Book Longevity of the Council on Library Resources, Inc. ∞

First published in 1994 by Viking Penguin, a division of Penguin Books USA Inc. First printing of the University of Oklahoma Press edition, 2001.

1   2   3   4   5   6   7   8   9   10

BALSAMROOT

/ / / / /

Also by the author

All But the Waltz (New York, 1991; paperback, Norman, 2001)

Bone Deep in Landscape (Norman, 1999)

(ed.) *Circle of Women: An Anthology of Western Women's Writing*, with Kim Barnes (New York, 1994)

Lambing Out and Other Stories (Columbia, 1977; paperback, Norman, 2001)

Runaway (Lewiston, 1990)

Sister Coyote (New York, 2000)

(ed.) *Written on Water: Essays on Idaho Rivers* (New York, 2000) *for Brian*

BALSAMROOT

/////

1

/ / /

My aunt had chosen her place well. She owned two large lots, heavily overgrown with alder and blackberries and firs, on a promontory outside Port Angeles, Washington, where for forty years she lived alone in a house overlooking the blue haze of the Strait of Juan de Fuca. My aunt kept a pair of binoculars on her windowsill and learned to identify the ships that moved slowly up and down the strait with their loads of logs and woodchips, and she learned the moods of sky and water, the way the fog rolled in and isolated her house on its scrap of lawn, the days of slanting gray rain that froze on her road in the winter.

My aunt's property edged a precipice which dropped a thousand feet down to Morse Creek and from there to the breakers. At her back rose the massive peaks of the Olympic Mountains, closing off the rest of the continent. From her window, if the fog lifted at night, she could see the lights of Victoria, Canada, across the strait, thirty miles away. Only a Coast Guard station on a thin curving spit of land lay between her and the Pacific Ocean; she had come as far west as she could, to the very outermost reach of the Olympic Peninsula.

I visited my aunt perhaps a dozen times over twenty years, more often than anyone else did. Once I stayed a week with her. I was trying to gird myself to go back to my husband. She was still teaching in Port Angeles at that time. She would leave for school in the early mornings, closing the front door quietly behind her, while I half-woke in her spare room and then dozed through the hours, aware of the thin light and silence around me.

By four o'clock I would have managed to pull myself together and get dressed. Then I would hear the car on the gravel drive, the rumble of the garage door, and my aunt would be coming through the entryway with rain sparkling on her coat and scarf, laughing and defending her good nylon stockings from her excited little dog, who also had slept away the hours of her absence.

I know her kitchen as well as I do my own by now, and I have started a casserole of rice and chunks of salmon from a neighbor's fresh catch and the grated cheese I salvaged from a moldy bar at the back of her refrigerator. My aunt doesn't really like wine, but she has bought a bottle for me. She'll have a cigarette, instead, after she has changed clothes. She is thankful to be home. Her dog patters after her, leaps into her lap when she sits down.

Can I recall her as clearly as I do the astringent taste of that white wine, sipped from a jelly glass that really should have been washed, it had stood so long in the cupboard above the stove? My aunt at this time is in her late fifties, stout and vigorous from years of all-weather gardening. Nothing ever fazes her. In her house I am still her cherished little niece.

Smoke rises as she draws on her cigarette and exhales, her dark eyes sharp and ironical behind her glasses, her legs crossed in the worn-out dark rayon dress she favors for wear around the house. Her thick dark hair is cut and styled now, and streaked with gray, but it still curls as it did when she wore it in a braid around her head and rode horseback through the river breaks of central Montana with my mother and father, and her laugh still bursts out at almost anything. To me she looks the same as she always has, like Auntie, Auntie who came for the long summer visits when I was a child on that Montana ranch, and woke up our lives with the tang of elsewhere.

What I know of my aunt's youth is buried in the boxes and boxes of unsorted photographs stacked in the closet of her spare room. She laughs and says she really should label all these pictures, then tells me the names of faces which I instantly forget. She knows stories about the great-grandparents, cousins, distant connections from nineteenth-century Iowa or New York State. As the snapshots gradually progress to Montana in the early twentieth century, her stories get sparser; she has no narrative that will contain her parents, posed in the wavering grass of their homestead in 1910. Names are what she tells me. This is herself as a child, posed on the woodpile in elaborate ruffles and ribbons. This is herself at seventeen, going off to normal school in a plain jumper and shoes and hose. This is my mother, this is my father. These are the horses they rode. Long-dead horses. Their names. Pardner. Pet. Midget. Beauty. Dolly.

I am always struck by the stark backgrounds of those photographs. No trees, only the blistered siding of a two-room house casting its sharp shadow across bunchgrass or snow on the ground, and barbed-wire fences strung between sky and horizon. Not a landscape for the faint of heart. But my aunt and my mother and father knew nothing else. They were the first generation of Montana-born homestead children—my aunt was born in 1910, my father in 1913, my mother in 1914. Their parents had been on the land only a few years, and they were still hopeful. Later they would break sod and see their plowed fields blow away and their crops perish in the dry twenties, the dirty thirties, and they would lose hope, but their Montana-born children would take adversity for granted, poverty as pervasive, and they would smile for the box cameras, as proud of their horses and proud of each other as though they had money in their pockets or whole shoes on their feet.

Except that my mother and father stayed in Montana, on the ranch, and my aunt left, and made this safe space for herself on the outermost rim of the continent. Drought and dirt ranching and the names of horses would seem to hold no meaning for her now, or for me.

Later my aunt and I will eat our meal in the living room, at a card table set up in front of the window, and listen to the foghorns and watch the pinpoints of lights from the ships moving on the strait. What will we talk about?

Not about my marriage, though at some point I have told her the gist of my situation. My aunt has never married, never pretends to know a thing about the affairs of the heart. Nor will she speak words of sympathy to me, for we both have been brought up by a stern code, an old unstated rule: *Never speak aloud of what you feel deeply.*

So we talk about the family. Speculate on the currents flowing between the generations.

"My mother only met her grandfather once, when she was seven," my aunt tells me, "but she remembered him perfectly. She knew he didn't like her."

My aunt digs out more of the old photographs, reminds me of the names of those faces faded almost into the sepia of their backgrounds. What existence they still possess is contained in her memory of stories told to her. Here is the fierce old gentleman of Canisteo, New York, who disliked the little girl brought all the way from Iowa to be shown to him. (He is my how-many-greats-grandfather?) And this pale child in short pants and jacket, leaning against his mother with his ears sticking out and his eyes like globes, is the little boy cousin he liked better than he did my grandmother.

"I've always believed that Ma had great determination, even as a child," says my aunt, "and her grandfather sensed it and disliked her for it. He knew she was stronger-willed than the little boy."

Then she remembers another story and laughs. "The little boy's mother told Ma's mother, *My one little boy is worth all your eight children put together.* Can you imagine one sister saying that to another? Of course, her son did become a minister. Of a very fashionable parish in Chicago."

We ponder what could have burned so deeply between those sisters that it had to be concealed behind the meaningless, vindictive words. Not a very horrible secret, perhaps, by the standards of our day. My aunt tells me another story, about a cousin around whom an odor lingered, down the years, in the way her name was bitten off and spat away. "When I asked Ma and Aunt Mable what was being covered up about her, they looked at each other and said they really didn't know, unless it was that she was an Early Rose."

Early Rose?

"It was their way of saying she was born before her parents were married nine months."

Mothers and daughters, sisters and cousins, feelings as constant and treacherous and full of flux as the tide itself. I am lulled out of my present misery by the endless motion of those lives before mine. My aunt is like an ark, rocking with the weight of their fragments, their disconnected tales, the names written only in her head.

And yet for all our talk I never know why my aunt has chosen to live alone out here on a scrap of land between a rain forest and the Pacific Ocean, or why she needs distance and gray water and the solitude of her own house and wild garden between her and her family. If she has secrets of her own, she has kept them for so long that perhaps even she has forgotten them.

We will talk until late, or we will read, and then she will go to bed, leaving me to prowl her bookshelves for a historical novel or a best-seller from the 1940s, still in its dust jacket, to sustain me through the night. In a few days I will be back in Montana, facing my husband, but I'll carry with me the feeling of her house, her few sticks of furniture, bathrooms full of cat boxes, bookshelves overflowing, dust and cigarette butts and cobwebs and smell of rain and silence like a secret to see me through chaos. Hers is a place of peace and squalor I can always come back to.

The sixties slide by, and the seventies. I didn't stick with my marriage, after all. Mine is the first divorce in the family. But my grandmother is dead now, and Great-Aunt Mable is dead—"We never told Ma and Aunt Mable you were divorced. They died without ever having to know," my aunt assures me.

The deaths of the two old women left a void for my aunt, a cessation of a rhythm. For years she had driven down to my grandmother's farm, near Seattle, whenever she had a break from teaching. She had given her summers to cutting back blackberry vines, spading Aunt Mable's garden, feeding my grandmother's chickens. Run their errands for them, paid their bills, worried over them. Now she is relieved of duty. Hers is the generation on the edge. And yet my aunt seems unchanged to me, although by the 1980s she has long been retired from teaching, and I have remarried and had another baby and begun to show the rough edges in my face.

Every summer she still comes on her Montana vacation, driving her own car with her dog on the seat beside her, spending a few days with my mother in Lewistown, then driving up to Havre to spend a few days with me. After I move to Idaho, she adds another loop to her map. Always, in June, her car pulls up and she climbs out, her hair snow-white but still thick and curly, her face more gnomelike than ever.

She does seem smaller, her doctor has made her lose weight to alleviate her high blood pressure. The first thing she always does is take her dog out back to piddle on the lawn. Then she unpacks her cigarettes, her quilt pieces, whatever she has brought along to read. No more show of emotion between us than if she had come back after a fifteen-minute errand.

"Well, hello."

"I've got the pot on, do you feel like a cup of coffee?"

"It wasn't a bad drive at all, this time. I ran into a little road construction near Ellensburg, was all."

Sometimes she has a story to tell me about her encounters on the road. The time she stopped for gas and let a couple of locals solemnly try to spin her a jackalope yarn. "Where do you think I grew up?" she finally asked them. "Have you ever heard of

Denton, Montana? Don't you know I'm an old homesteader's kid? Have you ever heard of a sidehill winder?''

Or the time she stopped to wait for a pilot car to guide her through a stretch of highway construction, and the sunburned flag-woman, stopping at her rolled-down window to exchange a few courtesies in the crackling heat, looked at her license plates and at her white hair and finally asked her, ''Does your family know how far you are from home?''

This story gives us both a laugh. Who can imagine my aunt asking anybody's permission for anything she decides to do?

On her June vacations, she always spends just a few days with me, and then she is ready to hit the road again. She is eager to return to her own place. Make up for all the time she spent away from it while she was taking care of my grandmother and Aunt Mable. She wants to be by herself again. Get at the weeds, thin out the autumn crocus, transplant the glads. See how the cats have kept over the summer, and whether the raccoons are still coming around to the kitchen door at night.

''I'm going to sell my place,'' she wrote to me in the fall of 1989.

''Why?'' I wrote back. (And would ask myself savagely again and again in the course of the next year: Why? The woman is seventy-nine years old, that's why! Did you think that, because you're still a fool and still need her, she was never going to age?)

''I want to feel closer to my blood kin,'' she wrote. ''I'm going to buy a house in Idaho, near you. If that's all right with you.''

''It's certainly all right with me,'' I wrote back. ''I'll be glad to have you living near me. I've never had you to myself long enough. But why the hurry?''

Had I missed a cue, I wondered later? But if her letter had

contained an encoded request, it had been too delicate in its nuances for me to hear it. My aunt continued to write every few weeks as she always had, reporting on her gardening, the fog, the rain that had fallen as she walked to her mailbox, the extra cat that turned up on her doorstep one morning. And yet she returned to her insistent theme: *I'm going to sell my place.*

In midwinter she called me on the telephone, long distance. "Mary, I want to sell my house, but I don't know exactly what I ought to *do.*"

"Well—you should talk to several realtors—have you had it appraised?"

"No."

"You need to get an idea of what property out on the peninsula is selling for, and pick a realtor, and then give her the listing."

A silence.

"I just don't know," she repeated, unhappily. "Mary, my furnace gave out. It made a big oil leak on the floor."

"Have you had it fixed?"

"Oh, yes. Sort of. But it won't last forever."

"But you've got heat in the house?"

"Oh, yes."

"Look, I'm in the middle of my semester," I said finally, wondering what was going unspoken in her long pauses. "If you'll wait until June, I'll drive out to Port Angeles and help you put the place on the market. We can make a little holiday out of it. Drive around the peninsula, maybe take the ferry over to Victoria—"

"That would be lovely," she said. But behind her agreement was a resistance I could sense all the way through the long-distance line, and I hung up the phone feeling disquieted.

A week later she called again. "I've sold my house!"

"Already? How much was the appraisal?"

"Oh—well, I didn't get it appraised. I've sold it to John. He's going to take care of everything for me."

"Who's John?"

"Oh, he's a friend. I taught him in school. It's going to work out real well," she assured me. "John's got plans for my place. He's going to build a house on my other lot. I'll finance him, and—"

"You're going to *what?*"

As I dragged out of her the details of her transaction—no payments or interest required of John for the first year, well, because she wanted to give him a good *start;* no, she hadn't talked to a lawyer, because she didn't *know* any lawyers; well, she did know a lawyer, but she didn't know where his office was—I grew angrier and angrier, and she grew more and more distressed. But she wasn't budging.

"John and I are going to be working together on this deal," she kept saying. "And I don't want you telling anybody else in the family about it."

How do you keep your aunt from selling her house to a friend? Especially when she has already sold it? I would be reading or grading papers in my office, half-hearing the sounds of the campus—the voices of students outside my window on their way across the street to the tennis courts, the hum of the laser printer next door, the familiar chatter in the hall—and I would find my mind adrift: this must be why families swoop down on their elders with attorneys and restraining orders and frantic claims of mental incompetence. But what, if anything, is my plain duty? My aunt has asked me not to betray her confidence. She has never betrayed one of mine.

Worrying about her, I remind myself of my grandmother and Aunt Mable. *Some man might want to marry her yet!* they used to warn each other. *For her money!*

What if, worst come to worst, this John somehow cheats her out of the whole price of her house? Right now she is relishing the feeling that she is in business with him, that she is giving him a boost. Would it be any different if she had decided to sell the place and spend the proceeds on a trip around the world? Or if she'd decided to take it all to Las Vegas and gamble with it?

But none of my rationalizations matters. My aunt has made up her mind, and I have already come up against her adamance. *I don't know any lawyers,* stated as an irrefutable conclusion. *Quod erat demonstrandum.*

On the west side of the Continental Divide, at the confluence of the Snake and Clearwater rivers, the mountains flatten out into the gray bluffs that shelter Lewiston, Idaho. Two hundred and fifteen miles to the east, over the Lolo Pass, is Missoula, Montana, and three hundred miles to the west is Seattle. Annual rainfall here is about eleven inches, and by August the hills lose any tinge of green and settle for the rest of the year under a stark pattern of shadows on the thick blond grass. Sometimes in the winter we see snow on the tops of the hills and far off on the mountains, but snow rarely falls here in the deep cleft of the rivers. We are a valley of dust and slow pewter-gray current and stinking white emissions from the Potlatch mill upriver.

When I came here to teach at the state college in 1987, the

river bluffs at first seemed forbidding to me, and then like familiars. Now I tried to imagine how those striated dry cliffs would seem to my aunt after her years of rain and cold breakers and her endless view of the strait. She would be changing elements, water for earth, and she would be bumping into me. I had not lived with a man for six years, had not lived within hundreds of miles of any relatives except my own children for twenty years, nor had she for forty years.

"John's going to drive me over from Port Angeles to look at houses," my aunt told me over the phone. "I want him to look them over for me before I make up my mind. You know how a *man* looks at a house."

"Yes," I said, irritated, "and a woman, too."

And she giggled, unsure of my tone.

But it gave me a chance to meet John when he pulled up in my driveway in a pickup truck with my aunt beaming beside him on the seat, although it had been a nine-hour drive, down the peninsula from Port Angeles, across Puget Sound by slow ferry, and then three hundred overland miles across Washington to Idaho.

John turned out to be a lively fellow in his forties, looking a little like one of the Super Mario Brothers in bib overalls and a black handlebar mustache.

"I wouldn't do anything to hurt Miss Welch," he assured me; and, seeing his gentleness with her, watching her bask in his affection, I felt less suspicious of him.

The house my aunt liked best stood on a hill overlooking the river, just a few blocks above mine. Carpeted and characterless, it seemed to me a sad trade for the house in Port Angeles, but it had a big back yard with fruit trees and a place for a garden, and from its deck my aunt could look down on the slow molten current of the Snake River where it flowed into the Clearwater, or she could look up at the bluff behind the house and watch the shadows move across its rock outcroppings.

John solemnly went over the house, examining its siding and foundations, asking questions about its construction and insulation, finally pronouncing it fit.

"Now I want you to take me to a bank," said my aunt, so I drove her to the branch I used and sat down in the lobby with a book to wait for her to open her new accounts. After a few minutes the bank officer called me over to her desk.

"We need you to sign here."

"Why?"

"I'm putting your name on all my accounts," explained my aunt, "just the same as Ma and Aunt Mable did when they put my name on their accounts."

And so, everywhere the bank officer had checked for the savings account, the checking account, the safety-deposit box, I signed my name under my aunt's. *Imogene Welch* in her large wavering script, *Mary Blew* in my much smaller and controlled hand.

Next we met the realtor at the title company to close on the new house. The realtor looked bemused as my aunt carefully wrote out a check for the full amount of the purchase.

"There's nothing much to closing on a house when you're paying cash for it," she remarked to me.

I felt as bemused as the realtor. On a teacher's salary, my aunt had saved enough to buy a new house outright without counting on the money from the sale of her old house. And I now knew enough about her remaining assets to feel certain that, if she never collected a payment from John, she would have ample income to "see her through," as she put it. In all her life, my aunt had never bought a single item on the installment plan, never borrowed money except once, from Aunt Mable, to build her first house. It had been years since she had spent an unnecessary penny on herself.

We are finished. My aunt can move into her new house in June. Meanwhile she will go back to Port Angeles with John, to pack her belongings. But before she leaves, she tells me a secret.

"I had a funny turn last fall. It was real spooky at the time. I got up in the morning, same as always, and took the dog for her walk, but when I got back to the house, I went in the kitchen and started to make oatmeal for my breakfast, and I couldn't remember how."

I don't quite take in what she is telling me. "What do you mean, you couldn't remember?"

"I just didn't know how. I couldn't figure out why the oatmeal wasn't cooking. It was just sitting there in the cold water."

"What did you do?"

But she draws back, tosses off her own story. "I made toast for my breakfast instead!"

What happens when the mind starts to wear out? I imagine the process as a dissolving of the layers between memories, like a wad of old photographs beginning to grow together. Where is my blue sweater, surely it should be in this drawer? But I can't find it, though my hands remember its exact texture, its slight cling at my fingers. Frantically I rummage through other drawers. What have I forgotten? One of my favorite sweaters. Could I have left it at the cleaners, *how long ago? Has it been years since I wore it?*

Or I imagine the process as the erasure of the line between past and present, until all experience exists simultaneously. Sometimes, between sleep and waking, I see the steep road through the tangle of blackberries and the sign, *Fresh Eggs for Sale,* and my grandmother's name on her mailbox, and it is as though I could still drive a little north of Seattle on I-405 and turn off on Bothell Way and, certain as a sleepwalker, find her old house at the other end of the tunnel of undergrowth and walk out into the sunlight where it falls on the two unpainted plank steps and open the screen door where the murmur of well-known voices resurrects oak chairs, wood stove, sagging floor. *What do you mean, there are no eggs for sale here anymore?*

Or I imagine my aunt falling through the hole in her mind. Coming to consciousness again in another time and place, in the smell of alkali and sagebrush, with nowhere to get out of the sun, with no sense of the future. Being twenty-five years old again and wanting to squirm with shame, wanting to crawl out of sight. Knowing from a younger sister's eyes that she knows my worst secret, and that she knows more she isn't telling. Having to ask her. *Where's my horse, where's Dolly? What do you mean, he stole her?*

Idaho is an enormous state: five hundred miles long and three hundred miles wide at its base; its panhandle juts off the spine of the Rockies with its face to the west. Until 1863, when the Territory of Montana was split off from the Idaho Territory, its area stretched beyond the imagination on both sides of the mountains. Even today Idaho is like an opposite facet of Montana, a kept secret in the shadow of Montana's glamour, its Sawtooths and Craters of the Moon and Big Lost River uninvented and unmythologized. "I always thought we lived in Montana," said a friend who grew up in the Salmon River country, the son of itinerant packers. "We got groceries in Montana and got our mail in Montana. We only came to Idaho to vote."

Driving from one end of Idaho to the other is often worse than driving across Montana. Idaho's highways are narrow and warped from deep frosts and thaws, and all its roads circle the edges of the great wilderness area that bulges out of the middle of the state. Often it's easier, if you want to go south, to cross over to the Montana side and from there continue down to Wyoming and Utah, or even to southeastern Idaho. Driving from Lewiston, at the base of the panhandle, down to Pocatello, in the southeast, takes twelve hours and a change of time zones, from Pacific to Rocky Mountain Standard Time. Nobody wonders why, although I have lived in Lewiston for three years, I never see my son in Pocatello, or my older daughter, who lives in St. Anthony, a hundred and fifty miles east of Pocatello, within sight of the Teton Range on the Wyoming border.

When Elizabeth does show up at my house in Lewiston, a few weeks after my aunt's visit, I hardly know her.

It isn't just the weight she has lost in the four or five years since I last saw her, but the absence of innocence in the drawn lines of her face. As we sit and talk through the lengthening spring twilight, watching the reflected lights begin to rise to the surface of the river, I remember how her cheeks stayed round even into her teens, and how long she kept her child's complacent certainty of all that was due her, even while she was being cheated of it. Can this grown woman with the fear and resolve in her eyes possibly be my daughter? Watching her, watching myself as I skitter around the deep waters, chatting with her as I would with one of my graduate students, I wonder why Elizabeth has driven all the way up from the Wyoming border, seven hundred miles alone with her dog, to see me after all this time.

And then Rachel bursts in.

Rachel is twenty-one years and one day younger than Elizabeth. She has seen nothing of her brother and little of her sister, she cannot remember the brief time when we all lived together, and she has been beside herself with curiosity and excitement ever since she heard Elizabeth was coming for a visit. How can it be, she has kept asking, that Elizabeth can remember her daddy, when she can't remember him herself?

Now Rachel hangs on the banister rail and giggles, won't come upstairs to the living room until she is coaxed. Elizabeth looks startled at all this attention from a seven-year-old. Her eyes widen and the cords in her neck bulge out. She really is much too thin. And her dog, a young blue heeler cross, hates children and leaps up, growling, whenever Rachel approaches. Before the weekend is over, I will have learned to leap up myself, and peel Rachel or one of her friends off the wall where Katy is holding her at bay.

"Dave and I are getting a divorce," Elizabeth says when she has the chance.

I absorb this news cautiously. Elizabeth seems calm. But the walls of my safe Idaho living room have turned transparent. I don't know this woman anymore, but I can remember when she was not much older than Rachel is now, and how my resolve shriveled and barely survived at the sight of the tears running down the face of the child on the other side of the kitchen table. *Your dad and I are getting a divorce.*

The fissures between past and present close at the edges. I remember too well how it felt to fall to pieces, I still feel the cracks across my face. Fingers and arms snatched away, skin peeled back, face liquefying—waking up at night on the brink, wanting to scream, not daring to scream, wanting out of my skin—no, I don't want to remember my disintegration, I don't want to keep living with Elizabeth's blame. I don't want to have anything more to do with her.

But later that evening, when Rachel has gone to bed and the house has quieted down, Elizabeth talks about her plans. She always wanted to be a veterinarian, worked for a vet all through high school, then went off to college and dropped out of the pre-vet program to get married. Finished her degree in teaching instead, went with her husband when he took a job in rural southern Idaho.

Then something happened—something carved the confidence out of her face. She resolved to go back to the beginning, to apply for vet school. *Not and stay married to me,* her husband said, and that was that.

Now she has been working as a vet's assistant down in southern Idaho, will do the same here, work without pay if she has to, whatever it takes to show the vet faculty at Washington State University in Pullman that she is serious this time.

"I'm going to move up here to Lewiston," she says. "Pullman is only thirty miles up the road. I'll find a place to live and get a job and keep applying until they take me. If that's all right with you," she adds carefully, just as my aunt did.

First my aunt and now Elizabeth, what is this? The face of the unhappy child surfaces under the features of this near stranger like a double exposure. Am I really her mother?

In turn, hoping for safe conversational footing, I tell Elizabeth about Auntie's big plans. "I have to drive out to Port Angeles as soon as the semester is over," I explain. "She thinks she can't pack her dishes by herself."

Elizabeth's face lightens. Like all the children, she has always loved Auntie. "I'll go with you," she volunteers. "For the ride."

2

/ / /

*Why leave home? Why pack your car with every-*thing it can hold, including your child, who is not quite five, and two sedated cats, and head west? Why did you take that deep breath when you saw the *Welcome to Idaho* sign in your headlights at the top of Lolo Pass, and you knew you were crossing the state line? A Montana warrant can't keep you from taking your child to Idaho with you now.

Ahead of you in the dark, disappearing around the corkscrew curves of Highway 12, are the winking red brake lights on the horse trailer your brother-in-law is hauling to Idaho for you. Your car and the horse trailer and the truck your brother-in-law is driving contain everything you possess.

"If you get even the slightest inkling that he might have gotten a court order," my sister told me, "what you should do is take

Rachel and leave with her before they can serve the papers on you. We have a friend who will meet you in Great Falls and take your car and let you take his. You'll have Cascade County license plates and enough start to get over the Idaho line before anybody catches on. We'll be on the road behind you somewhere.''

That was the fall of 1987. There had been no court order, only the memory of the sick and angry man left behind. Two marriages behind me now. But I was able to start teaching in peace at the state college in Lewiston, dropping Rachel off at the campus day-care center in the mornings and picking her up in the afternoons. Safe behind the illusion of boundaries, watching the light change patterns on the massive face of the Lewiston Hill, learning the grid of streets and the searing fall sunlight on the downtown intersections, learning how to find the public library, how to find the dentist's office, how to find the dry cleaner's, I stopped thinking about the endless curves and twists and blind corners on Lolo Pass between me and Montana.

In the fall of 1989 I drove up to Coeur d'Alene, Idaho, to present a paper at a professional conference. Brilliant sky, brilliant sun on lake water, red leaves falling everywhere, and a red message light winking in my hotel room. His sister's voice on the other end of the phone. Over in Montana, Rachel's father had died of the wasting disease that had gradually eaten away his muscles and his reason.

So that was that.

Now, in June of 1990, the day after Rachel has finished the first grade, she and I and Elizabeth get into my car and head west. We cross the Snake River into Washington, follow Highway 12 past

Pomeroy, then turn off toward Lyon's Ferry, and cross the river again. The narrow potholed asphalt winds and climbs up through dirt bluffs and sagebrush to emerge on the plains of central Washington. Another hundred and fifty miles and we will meet the Columbia River on its way south and cross over to I-90 for the rest of the way to Seattle. In the eyes of passing tourists or truckers, we are two women in blue jeans, one small girl with a blond braid to her waist, and one frightened blue dog.

Katy huddles on the floor of the car at Elizabeth's feet and shakes. She doesn't have an idea in the world what is happening. When Rachel leans too far over the back seat, she snarls at her.

I think of how many times Auntie must have driven this road, how much sagebrush she must have seen, and how many miles of wheatland and barbed-wire fence. The first time would have been in September of 1942, in a car loaded with everything she possessed, including a pair of crutches. She had just turned thirty-two years old, and she bore a fresh red wound around her right ankle where, in a haying accident that June, the sickle bar of a horse-drawn mowing machine had eaten nearly to the bone. Her whole leg must have ached. She had been out of the hospital barely a month, she still could not get a shoe on her right foot, and she was driving a 1939 Ford with a stick shift and a clutch. She was on her way out of Montana to her first teaching job on the Olympic Peninsula.

I wonder what she did with her horses. Sold them, most likely.

Elizabeth says little. She watches the sagebrush roll past the car window, and I don't ask what she is thinking about, or what it was like to drive away from that small house in the shadow of the Tetons, with its barn and corrals. She left her horses with her ex-husband when she came north.

"One of the things that happened to me after I got married," she remarks, "is that I started to be afraid to drive by myself."

Driving in the West means distance. All of us do it, at seventy or eighty miles an hour for hours on end, on the way to our next conference or workshop or connection with friends. What is behind us rolls back with the hundreds of miles of hardly any traffic and plenty of horizon. Time shrinks behind us. Nothing seems more essential than piles of clouds and hawks waiting for movement out of the shadows, oblivious to me and my thoughts as landscape eases out of the gray grass and bleached rock of central Washington into the long timbered climb over Snoqualmie Pass and the green descent into soft coastal rain.

Rachel and Elizabeth and I stay overnight at Aunt Sylva's and Uncle Ervin's in Seattle, then make a late start to catch the Edmonds ferry. No real hurry, after all. Long-distance driving means escape from time. Auntie is expecting us for dinner. We'll pack her dishes and have tomorrow and the next day on the peninsula. Meanwhile the sights and sounds of the dock at Edmonds are the same as always: the lines of cars waiting for the ferry, the newspaper hawkers, the gulls nesting on pilings, and the sailboats as far out as birds on this narrow neck of Puget Sound.

When the sun breaks out, I roll down the car window and lean back and watch for the ferry churning back from Kingston with its wake spread out behind it. Now, smelling the salt under the stink of creosote and rotting fish and diesel fuel, listening to the filthy green water lap at the planks under us, I am wafted out of myself. Reaching the peninsula for me has always been like shedding a skin. Maybe I can start over with the silent woman beside me in the car.

Rachel can hardly wait until I have driven into the depths of the ferry, parked bumper-to-bumper, and set the emergency brake so she can hop out of the car and race up the several flights of metal stairs to the observation deck, where she will lean over the rail to feel the salt wind and watch the wake. Elizabeth watches her face, and I know she is reliving her own first trips to Auntie's house—*and who was that young woman, taking that other little girl across on the ferry? Was she really me?*

On that night, in my living room above the Snake River, when Elizabeth accused me of abuse, all I could say was, "I'm sorry." I couldn't remember the day she remembered, or the wooden spoon I seized in my rage, or the serious welts she says I raised on her legs and back. She's the one who has to live with the recollections. Depression after my divorce erased my young womanhood. Often I come up against blank spaces, whole pieces missing, until I feel almost certain that Rachel is the only child I ever had.

And then we're driving off the ferry at Kingston, over miles of sunlight slanting through firs where time stops and roads disappear into the forest like tunnels. Impossible to believe that we are driving into the twenty-first century and that nothing is as pristine as it seems. We get glimpses of log booms on water, catch the scent of fresh-cut sawdust and turpentine. Take the sharp turn at Port Gamble, slow down for the trim white picket fences and carefully restored frame houses of nineteenth-century sea captains and settlers. Then more water, sparkling and calm under the Hood Canal bridge. More forest. Next will be Sequim. After Sequim, Port Angeles. Rachel's getting tired. I'm getting tired. The dog has gone to sleep.

At last, in the late afternoon, we turn off the highway and take the familiar turn onto the point and down the overgrown driveway, past the fruit trees and the row of marionberry bushes and the weedy beds where the irises used to grow.

At the sound of the car, Auntie dashes out of the house to meet us. Camera freeze: how can I forget that first glimpse of her face, altered under the mop of white curls? Even the deep weather-beaten folds and wrinkles seem to have ironed themselves out. A curious blankness of the eyes, a stranger's stare.

The moment passes.

"I see you made it," she says. She sounds almost like herself. And she looks almost right. She is bone-thin, her skin hangs on her arms in ropy folds, but she is agile from her years of gardening and long morning walks. I'm tired, my mind balks. I tell myself that all I saw was the effect of this upheaval on a woman who is almost eighty.

In the shadowed entryway I stop again, noting details. The telephone table is still in the hall. The hundred-pound sack of dogfood that she keeps to feed the raccoons is half-in, half-out of the tiny front bathroom. For years it has been impossible to shut that door. Through the archway I see a crazy assortment on the dining-room table. Old fruit jars, stemmed goblets, packets of dry soup mix, pots and pans, condiments, and canned catfood. The living-room floor is stacked nearly to the ceiling where somebody has pulled most of the books off the shelves and packed them in boxes. Cobwebs, clutter, smoke stains, and the smell of cats and stale cigarettes, but, except for the books, no attempt at packing.

Then my aunt's stone-deaf little dog wakes up to our alien presence and erupts out of her chair, barking and snarling. Startled at this noisy wad of dirty white hair, Elizabeth's dog stiffens and growls.

"Shellie! Shellie!" my aunt cries, trying to save her darling as cats flee and we drag Elizabeth's dog outside and tether her to the garage.

Out of earshot in the late sun, where a few gone-to-seed pansies hang on in the flowerboxes, Elizabeth gives me a stricken look. "How long has her house been like this?" she whispers.

I shake my head. Auntie's housekeeping has always been casual, dust has never concerned her, but I was here last summer, and there were no pockets of gray cobwebs as deep as my wrists, no smell.

"Of course, any house looks awful when you're moving out of it," I remind Elizabeth, and she nods tentatively.

"But it's going to take *weeks,*" she says.

Back in the house, my aunt is cuddling her little dog, trying to console her.

"I take it we're not going to have dinner here tonight?" I ask, and she looks at me blankly.

Actually, the packing and cleaning of Auntie's house takes us three days. Elizabeth and I pitch in without further discussion, and Rachel pitches in beside us. When I visit the liquor store in Port Angeles in search of empty cardboard boxes, Rachel staggers back and forth to the trunk of the car, carrying stacks of boxes higher than she is. Back at Auntie's house, she works without complaint, drags garbage bag after garbage bag out to the growing mountain on the front lawn for John and his father to haul off later. Every time she trudges past one of the dogs, it snaps at her.

My aunt trots around, dazed, giving me contradictory answers as to what to pack, what to throw away, until finally I stop asking. But I wonder, What in the world is going on in this woman's head? John and his father are going to drive everything over to Idaho in a U-Haul for her, but surely she knows she has to stow her breakables. I feel an unreasoning irritation with her. On her desk sits a glass bud vase with a dusty artificial rose stuck in it. How, I wonder, glowering at it every time I walk by, does she expect *that* arrangement to make the trip?

"My pets live here, too," I remember her saying years ago, "and I'm not going to keep a house so fine that they don't feel comfortable in it."

Now Elizabeth holds the garbage bag open while I toss in the countless motheaten sweaters, the countless blankets matted with the hair of Shellie's predecessors, the dozens of carpet samples that have been strewn around the house for animals to relieve themselves upon. ("And whatever became of that gray sweater, the one I kept behind the chair for Shellie? I just can't *find* it," my aunt will fret, weeks and months from now.)

Elizabeth and I don't quite meet each other's eyes as into the garbage bag go the plastic margarine tubs that have been deployed everywhere to hold animal food and drink, the plastic tubs the cottage cheese came in, the wastebasket made of Styrofoam egg cartons laced together with fluorescent yarn. In snatched moments out of earshot we decide what to do with broken chairs and endless empty peanut-butter jars, and I hear my aunt's voice from years ago—*Ma and Aunt Mable hover over us until Sylva and I have to go out to the garden to get a private word in.*

Boxes of family pictures, letters, magazines, Bibles. Boxes of odds and ends. Seventy handmade quilts. Boxes of LP records.

A complete album of the original Carter family, a dozen 78 rpms with red-and-gold labels shining out of the brown paper sleeves. My grandmother's china dishes. My aunt's silverware. What, I wonder, did a woman who so seldom entertained want with a complete set of sterling butter knives, Rosepoint pattern?

I feel like a voyeur, a prowler, a vandal of my aunt's secrets. "It was just dreadful," I remember her telling me about the time she and Aunt Sylva had to empty out my grandmother's house. "All the time Sylva and I were working, I could just hear Ma: *Now, you girls leave my things alone!*"

Elizabeth scours the bathrooms, scours the layers of grease and dust off the kitchen appliances. The refrigerator changes color, takes on a soapy gleam of racks and shelves. She says little, and, as I scrub down the kitchen cabinets and scrub the floor on my hands and knees, I wonder how far into her debt I'm descending. Why is she helping me? Why are we scrubbing this house, anyway? The linoleum, the countertops all need to be replaced, and John is going to come in and remodel, but at least we won't be leaving the place filthy.

I feel filthy. But when I catch sight of my own face in the bathroom mirror, my hair in wild strands, what I think of is the story of the mirror. It hangs on an unlit wall over the sink, one of those twelve-inch round mirrors from the 1950s with a swan etched into it, the only mirror in the house.

"Certain things just don't matter to her," Uncle Ervin had pointed out to me. "Appearances. Conveniences. The day I fin- ished building her house, I took that little mirror out of my camper and hung it in her bathroom for the time being, until she could pick out a better one. Forty years later, that mirror's still there.''

At night Elizabeth takes the couch in the living room while Rachel and I sleep in Aunt Mable's pickled-oak bed in the spare room. I lie awake in the dark and listen to the faint, alien sounds of the point, the calls of owls and rumble of faraway traffic. Rachel's soft breath rises and falls. Her bottom digs into my ribs, but if I move over any farther I'll be on the floor. But we're used to sleeping together. *Don't worry about it. She'll move back into her own bed when she's ready,* said the psychologist, and I hope he's right. She moved into my bed when her father left, and it's only lately that she has been sleeping in her own bed most of the time.

I'm so tired that my bones ache, but I can't sleep. How many times have I lain awake in this bed? The years drift back. What to do about Rachel's father. That moment I could not define, when I knew I was dealing with irrationality. Was it a lack of expression in his eyes? A glimpse of animal calculation?

Then a pale shape moves out of the verge of sleep at the bedroom door. It is Elizabeth—''Mother? Are you awake?''

''What's wrong?''

Her voice is shaking. ''Mother, do you have any idea how to get the cat out of the couch? He's up inside the frame, and he's been growling at the dog all night, and the dog growls back, and I can't sleep—''

How to get the cat out of the couch. I must have been deeper into a dream than I thought. I throw back the covers and plod after her in my nightgown. Rachel slides out of bed and tags right behind me, rubbing her eyes and blinking in the light, as I detour around the stacks of boxes in the living room. Sure enough, a deep aggrieved tomcat voice emanates from some crevice in the frame of the couch. And here's Katy, curled up at one end of the couch and looking guilty. And here comes Auntie out of her room in her nightgown to see what is going on.

I have no idea how to get the cat out of the couch, but I stand on the cushions in my bare feet and jump up and down as hard as I can. Dust and cat hair rise explosively. The poor old couch lurches, and the tomcat shoots out and disappears through the kitchen window. Everybody looks at me, surprised.

Then Rachel starts to laugh, laughs so hard she doubles over. "Mom, you look ridicklelus! How come you didn't ask me to jump on the couch so you wouldn't have to look so ridicklelus?"

"Well—" says Elizabeth, still looking surprised. "Thanks."

A glimpse of Auntie's face. Blank. This time I recognize what I am seeing.

John's mother, Phyllis, drops by the next morning to see how we're doing. Turns out that she's the one who packed all the books.

"Sure am glad to see you here, Mary!"

My aunt is delighted to see Phyllis. She digs a packet of forbidden cigarettes out of the junk on top of the refrigerator, and she and Phyllis both light up. I feel a pang at this glimpse of the tiny pleasures of my aunt's life, the small rituals I have had no part in, how much she is giving up to come and live near me.

Phyllis shakes her head over the state of the house. "I am glad to see you, Mary. She really trusts you, you know."

Then Phyllis tells me a little more about the "turn" my aunt had last fall. "When she couldn't remember how to cook her oatmeal? She called me, and I came over and took her to the doctor. By that time she seemed fine. I told the doctor I thought she might have had a stroke. He said, Are you a doctor? I said, No, but I've had a stroke myself. He said, She's a borderline diabetic, she's had a low-blood-sugar reaction, is all. We'll put her on Glucotrol.''

How much unobtrusive care has Phyllis been giving to my aunt, getting her to doctors' appointments, taking her shopping? Certainly there is little food in the house, and my aunt is thinner than I have ever seen her. Has she been living on toast and packets of soup mix? How much driving has she been doing? Once, when I ask her to move her car away from the front of the garage, she leaps in, throws it into reverse, and backs into the woodpile.

We work more and more feverishly, sorting and packing, taping and labeling boxes, taking time only for meals from the delicatessen section of the supermarket in Port Angeles, eaten standing up or sitting on the floor. On the morning we are ready to leave, two boys from the Salvation Army arrive to haul off the old couch, by prior arrangement with Phyllis. Auntie can hardly bear to see the dear familiar thing go, but, from the expressions on the boys' faces when they see where cat hair has grown into the upholstery and how the loose strands hang where claws have been sharpened on it, I have a feeling they'll head straight for the dump with it.

"I'll help you shop for a new sofa," I promise Auntie. But what does she care about a new one?

I catch myself lapsing into a callused kind of humor. Raccoons, dogs, cats, this place is a damned zoo.

My aunt's cats, unnerved already by the upheaval of their house-hold, are outraged at the intrusion of strangers with a strange dog. The old cat, Tinker Bell, simply vanishes into the woods. The big neutered male, Jick, crouches under the furniture and growls at the dogs all day long in an unforgiving baritone. Only Blueboy, the recently arrived Siamese stray, a nuisance if there ever was one, stays underfoot.

"How are we ever going to catch Tinker Bell?" I ask my aunt. "What if we can't catch her?"

"Oh, my neighbor will catch her for me. He has a cat trap." Auntie giggles. "He's not happy about my cats. I think he's caught Tinker Bell before, but he knows which cats are really mine, and he always lets her go."

I have no idea what she is talking about until months later, when I learn from John that she has been driving her neighbors crazy by feeding the abandoned pets, a starving population of thirty to fifty cats that have been dumped out here on the point by assholes from town. The man next door has been trapping cats, sorting out Tinker Bell, Jick, and Blueboy, and hauling the others to the animal shelter in Port Angeles. At least now I know why we found the dozens of empty margarine tubs around her house and garage.

Sure enough, in the morning the neighbor brings us Tinker Bell. She is a lovely long-haired gray tabby, tipped with black, fifteen or sixteen years old. My aunt cradles her, caresses her, reassured to hold this old companion in her arms.

Feeling like the farmer who had to ferry a fox, a goose, and a bag of corn across a river in a boat that would hold only two passengers, I consider the deployment of our little company for the drive back to Idaho. My aunt's dog cannot be separated from my aunt, nor Katy from Elizabeth. Katy hates Rachel. Rachel isn't crazy about Katy, but her feelings come nowhere near the intensity of my aunt's cats, who set up a yowl of outrage at the barest whiff of her. My aunt's dog hates everybody.

But at last we're ready to pull out of the familiar driveway forever, past the marionberry bushes and the fruit trees and the mailbox. In the rearview mirror, the pile of garbage bags on the front lawn looks as high as the house. I look back over the little convoy that I have somehow found myself the captain of. I have put my aunt in the front seat of my car, with her dog, cowering and surly, on her lap. The envelope of papers from her Port Angeles safety-deposit box is in the glove compartment, the box of silverware on the floor of the back seat. The trunk is full and the back seat is loaded to the roof.

Behind us, Elizabeth is driving my aunt's car. I can see her face through the windshield, pale and set. She's not looking forward to following me through the ferries and the freeway traffic; she's still afraid to be driving by herself. Well, she certainly got more than she bargained for on this trip. Will she ever speak to me again? But how could I have known? And what would I have done without her? Auntie couldn't possibly have driven her car all the way to Idaho by herself.

Rachel sits beside Elizabeth in the front seat of Auntie's car. Katy is crouched on the floor at Rachel's feet, both of them stiff with their proximity to each other. In the back seat are the two cat carriers, one with Tinker Bell, one with Jick and Blueboy. Every other cranny in the car is stuffed with something.

Elizabeth says later that Blue never shuts up. All nine hours from Port Angeles, Washington, to Lewiston, Idaho, negotiating the ferry, trying to keep my car in sight through six-lane Seattle traffic, depending on Rachel for a spotter—*"There goes Mother!"* —cutting in front of trucks, and diving for exits, she listens to that Siamese yowl.

No spare space in that car at all. If Rachel and the dog want to sleep, it has to be on top of each other. Contrary to anything I would have expected, the effect of that cramped nine-hour drive is to resolve Elizabeth's apprehensions of Rachel. And we never know Katy to snap at a child again.

The first thing I do when we get to Idaho and pull up in my driveway is to get out and unload the cat carriers from the back of the other car. A hoarse Siamese voice sings like a chainsaw caught on a knot. Cat hair billows through the wire mesh as I set the carriers down on the sidewalk. My aunt climbs out of my car and hurries around to greet her pets. Even though she is an old cat hand, something warns me to try to head her off.

"Don't let those cats out right away! We'll have to keep them shut up in the house for a few days to help them locate themselves."

I may as well have saved my breath. My aunt dives past me and throws open the door of one of the carriers. Old Tinker Bell spurts out as though she has been fired from a rifle, crosses the street in a gray streak, and vanishes into the foreign shrubbery of Idaho, never to be seen again.

3

/ / /

It's not as though I really live alone. I live with Rachel and the cats and lately this mutt, Bear, who sleeps on my bed. Sleeping with a dog! I'm as bad as Auntie, although Elizabeth was kind enough to tell me about the research that says single people who sleep with pets are better off psychologically than those who don't.

What is my typical day like, an adult student from the Center for New Directions asks me. I feel almost embarrassed to tell her. But, well, I get up early. Six. I make coffee and let Bear out, let him back in again, and read the papers and sew quilt pieces, another habit I picked up from Auntie. Shower and wake Rachel up for school, go to work myself and teach a couple of classes, hold office hours, come home in time to meet the school bus. Give Rachel her dinner, help her practice the violin. Plan on settling in for an evening of correcting papers or reading or writing. A stiff whiskey last thing at night while I listen to jazz on KWSU and look down on the lights reflected on the river.

As single mothers go, I feel quite fortunate. I have enough money. I like my work. I like my flexible hours. I read. Or I walk by myself on the levee and look at the river.

Yes, but do I like it? Lately I've been feeling restive.

Trying to locate myself in these sheer hills where I have come to live, I have been reading Nez Percé history, about the people who lived for thousands of years along the Clearwater, the Salmon, and the Snake. It's a mistake to think that this place was ever wilderness. Until they were driven out by white gold-seekers, families lived in winter longhouses in these quiet canyons and told their children the stories that linked their lives to landscape.

I have been particularly drawn to Yellow Wolf, whose path was the reverse of mine, and bloodier and more bitter. Yellow Wolf was one of the patriot warriors who fought at White Bird and at the Clearwater, who retreated across Lolo Pass to Montana and fought again at the Big Hole and fled and fought and fled north to that final desperate encampment of the Nez Percés, seven hundred miles from home. Yellow Wolf survived the battle of the Bear's Paw, only a few miles from present-day Havre, where I lived for so long. But he didn't surrender to General Miles at the Bear's Paw when Joseph and the others did. He escaped and, in an agony of homesickness, fought his way mile by bloody mile back to Idaho, where he found—nothing.

I was riding alone, knowing what was ahead of me, Yellow Wolf told a white friend years later. His companions had turned themselves in, and now he was riding alone through summer grass on a good horse, a stolen horse, to surrender and be hanged. He had come to believe that no bullet could kill him. But at least he could make a last defiant gesture and die a brave death on the gallows.

Then the places through which I was riding came to my heart. It drew memories of old times, of my friends, when they were living on this river. My friends, my brothers, my sisters! All were gone! No tepees anywhere along the river. I was alone.

After we brought her back from Port Angeles, my aunt stayed with me for a few days until John and his father could bring her furniture over in the U-Haul and she could move into her new house. What I noticed during those days was her uncharacteristic idleness. No book in her lap, no quilt pieces. She sat in an armchair and stroked her dog, or she followed me about. I found her behavior irritating, incomprehensible. Once, when I tried to sneak downstairs to my desk and do a little work on an unfinished manuscript, I felt a faint stir at my back and turned to find her standing there, watching me.

"Auntie, what do you need?"

No answer. She looked at me as blankly as though knowing what she needed was a responsibility she had delegated to me.

I sighed and switched off the computer, led her upstairs, and made fresh coffee for her. Settled in a chair, sipping coffee, satisfied now that she had my attention, my aunt rambled happily on one of her favorite topics, the hardships of the Montana homestead life of her childhood. I half-listened, half-drifted back to the paragraph I had been trying to revise. If I could only have an hour to myself, bring it to a conclusion—

"—yes, it was a good life, all right. While it lasted."

"What do you mean, it was a good life?" I am startled back into my aunt's story. "I thought you said it was a hard life."

"It was a good life because, in those days, people lived on what they earned."

"What do you think they live on now?"

"Most people live on *credit.*" She rolls the word around like a bad taste on her tongue, repeats it. "On *credit.*"

She irritates me out of all proportion. I grew up with that Depression-era ethic, too, and I've had to fight off the sanctimonious voices inside my head every time I applied for a car loan or set up housekeeping by myself or otherwise took my own chances. *Don't, don't, don't.* Don't risk anything, don't spend a dime; whatever you do, don't enjoy yourself. Now here I am with my life, and at least it's mine. In the peace and quiet of Idaho, I've been raising Rachel by myself, and teaching again after all those years in higher-ed administration, and finding time to write again.

And now my aunt is living on my *credit,* spending it lavishly while I can't get back to my desk. My time to write is in the summer, when I have no classes to teach and I can count on several uninterrupted weeks, and I resent intrusions. For years I've fended off my children's demands, even their needs, so I can write, and I've made all the little choices over the years—*no, I can't take the weekend off, my manuscript is at a point*—*no, I can't even linger on the phone.* I've sworn off men, hardly ever go out with friends.

And now this disruption of my household. I've taken Rachel back to sleep with me so Elizabeth can have Rachel's bed while Auntie shares my spare room with her hateful little dog that gnaws dog treats all over the bed and leaves her piles in the corners of the living room, and I can't even get back to my desk for an afternoon.

Trying for a total that will ease my conscience, I count up the hours my aunt has cost me. All the afternoons I have spent trailing through houses after the realtor, all the anxieties of the drive to Port Angeles, and then the arm-aching mess of her house, which she has never explained, never apologized for—and June is nearly over, and in July I have promised to drive her over to Montana to visit the rest of the family, I have *that* interruption still ahead of me—hours! Hours!

And when did my aunt's frugality turn to stinginess? She let me pay for the meals while we were in Port Angeles, and all the meals and gas on the way back to Idaho, never gave the slightest indication that some of the financial responsibility might be hers. I feel ashamed of how much I have resented this expense. But ever since we got back, I've had to juggle my own bills so I can hold out until my July paycheck.

So I'm more than relieved when John and his folks show up with the U-Haul. Now we can get Auntie moved into her own house, get us all back to normal. Her white head bobs in excitement as she darts back and forth, getting in the way, while John and his father wrestle the bed, the chests of drawers, the walnut dining-room table, and the walnut china cabinet across the lawn and through the front door.

"All your friends in Port Angeles want to know whether Imogene found herself a nice little house in Idaho," they tease her. "And we ask them, Did you say a nice *little* house?"

My aunt giggles, delighted. She sounds like herself again. Surely, when we get her settled in, she can relax and live in pleasure in this house, which is certainly too big for her, but which has a garage ten paces from its kitchen, no steps up to its front door, no stairs she needs to climb to bathroom or laundry room. Already she loves her kitchen window, which looks up at the sharp river bluff, etched with gullies and the paths of small private creatures. Hawks ride the wind currents above that bluff, and rabbits and grouse venture all the way down to the thin line of irrigated lawns as far as the golf course, and coyotes sing at night from the south, and Auntie can spend hours watching and listening.

Also, she has struck a deal with Elizabeth.

When she heard Auntie's and my plans to rent Auntie's base-ment bedroom to a college student so she won't be alone in that big house, Elizabeth had said, "What about me? I'm going to be a college student again."

"Yes!" said Auntie, pleased. "I'll like that. You and I have always gotten along fine together."

Now Elizabeth says, "You need to know that I've got a boy-friend."

Auntie says, "That's all right. He can move in here, too!"

It's no more than I would have expected from Auntie. But I'm surprised by Elizabeth's tone. I knew there was a man somewhere in the background, a musician, I think, down in Wyoming, but up until now her references have been casual—too casual?

"Luckily, he travels a lot, so I have plenty of time to myself," she remarked once, and I remember thinking, *Who but a daughter of mine would say such a thing?*

In exchange for her room, Elizabeth will run errands, shop for groceries, help out with the cooking. To my relief. Secretly I know that Auntie will never be able to drive herself around Lewiston, as we had all hoped, hoped that during daylight hours at least she would enjoy the small freedom of driving herself to supermarket, doctor's office, public library. But she who only last summer could explain the directions to my house to a traveling cousin, she who last Thanksgiving drove herself all the way down from Port Angeles to Aunt Sylva's house in Seattle, cannot now remember the streets, the turns on the way home.

"Well, sweetie," says John's father, hugging my aunt. She sparkles back at him, flirting. They have known each other for years. He tells us about the time when he was a young teacher in the Port Angeles junior-high school and confessed his worries about his classroom discipline to Miss Welch down the hall, who showed him her secret weapon, a size-16 tennis shoe in her bottom desk drawer. Just let your kids know you can always borrow Miss Welch's tennis shoe, she advised him.

Her laugh bubbles over. "But I never threw shoes at anybody! Never! No matter what they say!"

Her shoe-throwing is an old story that they all tell, a joke I have never understood, with its connections to that old life in Port Angeles that John and his folks are winding up and taking home with them as soon as they have folded their tarpaulins and bolted up the U-Haul. Once again I have been beguiled by a glimpse of my aunt as her friends have always seen her, and I am saddened to think of her retreat into the ranks of family.

I am distracted by Shellie's behavior. Trailing her leash, her white hair matted and sad, the little old dog wanders about the new living room, sniffing at the chair legs and the base of the china cabinet, pausing as though in thought. *Where am I? What has happened? How can the familiar be reassembled in this strange dimension?*

Shellie has taken to spending most of her time sleeping on my aunt's lap. She does not want to be caressed, even by my aunt. The slightest disturbance brings her awake, snarling. When my aunt sets her down on the floor, she hobbles over to her food dish, retrieves one of her miniature dog-treats, and brings it back to gnaw at my aunt's feet.

Thus far all is familiar. For years now, everyone in our family has been resigned to walking around crunching on the forgotten crumbs of dog treats for days after one of my aunt's visits with Shellie. *The Beast,* one of my sisters calls her, although a dog less beastlike than Shellie is hard to imagine. Shellie weighs perhaps eight pounds. She has black button eyes that peep through a top-knot of silky white hair that is supposed to be brushed daily and tied up in a fresh ribbon. *Michelle* is her kennel name, and my aunt has always been too embarrassed to tell any of us what she paid for her. Shellie has always refused all food except her special dog-treats, will not even sniff a sliver of roast chicken or lick melted ice cream from a dish.

Also, she has never really been housebroken, though my aunt hovers over her anxiously. "Shellie? Do you need to go outside?"

Up and down my aunt hops from her chair, trying to time her short outdoor excursions to Shellie's bowels. Sometimes she succeeds, comes back indoors beaming.

"Shellie was a good girl! She squatted!"

But after one of my aunt's visits, we have always checked the dark corners of our halls and bedrooms for Shellie's tiny piles, and we are careful where we step.

It is in her neglect of Shellie that I realize how much my aunt has changed. When did she stop taking her to be groomed regularly? Why doesn't she brush out that matted hair?

"I'll take Shellie down to the vet for her rabies shot," promises Elizabeth in her new role as driver and carrier.

But she is somber when she returns. "Mother, she hasn't been taking care of Shellie! The vet pulled two of her teeth, he said they were so badly abscessed that they were draining infection into her system. But the worst of it is, she has congestive heart failure. She can't last long."

"And I suppose he wants to be paid!" cries my aunt, indignantly, when she opens the vet's bill.

"Why am I the only one putting money in the grocery kitty around here?" my aunt complains. "And what's this bill for brakes?"

Elizabeth is fairly shaking by the time she gets me alone. "I thought I was doing her a favor! I took her dog to the vet—and it was the same thing with her car, it hadn't been serviced since she bought it, and I made an appointment and took it down—and all she did was scream about the bill! I think she hates me. What am I doing wrong?"

"We'll try to pay the bills before she sees them, after this," is all I can think to suggest. I have been placating, soothing, trying to will Auntie's living arrangement with Elizabeth to work. Because what if it doesn't?

Grim-lipped, Elizabeth goes back to housecleaning. I have never seen such perfectionism. Every drawer must be immaculate, every chair leg dusted and aligned. Elizabeth polishes windows, shampoos the carpets right behind Shellie, vacuums Shellie's crumbs out of the arms of chairs, lines up the canned goods on the shelves with the labels facing in the same exact direction, and folds the laundry with mathematical precision. Every closet must be subdued, every cranny cleaned. She is driving Auntie crazy.

But when Elizabeth goes back to southern Idaho for a few days to collect her own belongings, my aunt rattles around her empty house, calls me several times a day.

"Mary? I can't find Shellie's leash."

"Mary, I don't know how to work this stove."

"Mary, there's a *fire* up here."

She can't keep track of her house key, locks herself out repeatedly. One morning, at first light, I am awakened by the doorbell, and I stagger downstairs with my robe half on, catching a glimpse of the clock—four-thirty, for godsake—and on my doorstep is a strange young woman. A truck is parked behind her in my driveway.

"I have your aunt with me," she says, and sure enough there is Auntie, grinning out the window of the truck.

"I took Shellie out to piddle and couldn't get back in my house," she explains, perfectly unabashed, as she climbs out of the truck in her nightgown and bare feet. "I didn't know what to do, but then this girl came along. She delivers the *Tribune*."

"I had to finish my route," says the young woman, "but I couldn't leave her alone. So I put her in the truck with my kids and took her along. She's been riding around with us for an hour."

"She was a real nice girl," says my aunt, after I have led her upstairs and made her a cup of coffee. "She had a two-year-old and a tiny baby, and she was taking them around on the paper route with her. She was real good to me."

In July, in spite of my apprehensions, I drive my aunt over to Montana for her summer visit with my mother. The trip goes well, although as always, after we leave Great Falls and cut through the wheatfields on poor battered Highway 87 into Fergus County, the landmarks start to bear down and I feel suffocated. The missing towns. The empty place on the hill where the Duck Creek School used to stand, where my father finished the eighth grade, where Auntie taught for three years just before she left Montana for good, where I went to school from fourth to seventh grade. From the road I can see the familiar outline of the South Moccasin Mountains and the soft foothills where my aunt and my mother once rode twenty hours looking for horses. My mother was married by then, and the story goes that she was pregnant with me, and she was riding my father's top horse, Pardner, and my aunt was riding Dolly.

Names of horses. Trivia. Details no one else can ever know or care about. *Buck* was the name my father called me, and Buck was also the name of the catch mare, the chore horse. I started riding Buck the summer I was thirteen, and I rode her hard every summer after that until I was seventeen, when I left home. She was part thoroughbred, not broken until a four-year-old, and then spoiled, so she'd never stand for a rider, but broke from standing to a gallop; one toe in the stirrup had to be enough. And she fretted and tore at the bit, iron-mouthed, wanting to run. She could never stand to be petted, but she would lead anywhere—she followed me through the thornbrush in the milk-cow pasture, dipping her head down under branches, snapping off pine stubs and jerking the saddle horn through spines and thorns that tore at each other while I crawled ahead of her in my father's Levi jacket and leather chaps in hundred-degree heat—and she found the way home for me at night through blackened pines when all the trails looked alike in the dark.

My father never got over my defection from the ranch. But the

girl left, the chore horse died. And who, to look at Auntie and
me now, could guess we ever knew the names of horses? A tired
woman in her middle years, putting another thousand miles on
her car, and the white-haired woman in the seat beside her with
the blank eyes and the little dog shivering in her lap. Neither of
us has ridden a horse in years.

But the trip goes well. Auntie has always been a good traveler,
and we spend our few uneventful days at the ranch. Neither my
mother nor my sister notices a change in her—"Except," says
my sister afterward, "that she seemed so quiet. And once I caught
an expression on her face—she was just sitting there, in Mother's
kitchen, and she looked, I don't know, *afraid*. I wonder now if
she knew where she was."

On the way home, on the Idaho side of Lolo Pass, I spot some
river rafters below us on the Lochsa and pull off the highway on
a gravel verge to let Rachel watch them shoot the rapids. Auntie
gets out of the car, too, carrying Shellie under her arm, and we
all lean over the guard rail to watch the rafters.

It is one of those heavenly spaces of pine breeze and ripe grass
at the top of the Continental Divide, mountain peaks rising on all
sides, the highway disappearing around the next hairpin turn, the
river roaring at the bottom of the precipitous drop. Just below us
the rubber raft is bucking and diving through the spray with its
load of shrieking rafters like a cargo of sensations shooting through
the afternoon. The rafters know we're watching, they wave, and
Rachel jumps up and down and waves back, leans far over the
guard rail to catch a last glimpse as the raft rounds the next bend,
the shrieks die away, and all that remains is the roar of the current.

I feel a little bereft. To feel spray in my face again—

"Time to go," I tell Rachel. "Time to get back in the car," I repeat for Auntie's benefit.

Auntie looks blankly at me. It's the look I've come to recognize, and yet more so; I could swear she doesn't know the car is parked there, or even what the word *car* means. What has happened in these two or three minutes? The sun beats down on the grass and gravel and her white head as she stands there, clutching her dog.

"Get back in the car, Auntie."

I take her elbow and turn her around, and she does get into the car, but on the driver's side, under the steering wheel.

"Auntie, you have to move over so I can drive."

I'm not sure she can see me, but apparently she can hear my voice, even has an idea what my words mean, because she shifts over an inch or two on the seat. When I push her the rest of the way over to the passenger side and buckle her in, she doesn't exactly resist, but neither does she cooperate. Rachel slips into the back seat. Her eyes are wide and scared.

Nothing is in sight but the river and the pines. This is the Clearwater National Forest, after all, and we are eighty miles from the nearest town. But the only thing I can think to do is get us down the pass. I pull off the gravel verge and start down those eighty winding miles.

The river rushes along below us, and the pavement flickers with alternating bars of sun and the shadows of pines. Deep summer grass grows between the boulders above the road, and the colors of the season, yellow balsamroot and paintbrush and wild geranium, bloom out of the crevices, and mountain bluejays flash out of the aspens, vanish, and reappear as though this slow July afternoon will never come to an end.

"You'd think," says Auntie, breaking the silence hoarsely, "that somebody in one of these houses could tell us where we *are*."

"What houses?" says Rachel. "Auntie, there aren't any houses up here!"

Auntie doesn't answer. She is mumbling to herself and holding Shellie so tightly that the old dog squirms to get away. Occasionally I make out fragments of her inner discourse: "—it was a round house, and all the children ran around and around it, looking for a way out—"

"What house was that, Auntie?"

Long pause before she answers, as though over centuries. "My uncle's house, I think."

For once this road seems empty of its summer traffic, no vans pulled over to disgorge rafters and rafting gear, no trucks with stockracks and loads of saddle horses, no carloads of fishermen. The Lochsa River descends and froths along with us as I take the curves at seventy miles an hour and my aunt mutters and rambles and stares through the windshield at a spectral world. Rachel is absolutely silent in the back seat.

We are still a hundred miles from Lewiston, still in the national forest, when the Lochsa spills into the Clearwater and the little settlements begin to crop out on the north side of the highway, wherever there is a level space carved out of the side of the mountain. Lowell. Syringa. Gas pumps and *45 mph* warnings and hand-lettered signs. *Wild game processed here. Wild huckleberry pies for sale here.* Motorcycles propped around the porch of the café, pickup trucks parked, an everyday world going on outside the sick, sealed capsule of my car.

When I park by the motorcycles, Auntie refuses to get out of the car, won't budge, clamps her mouth shut at the suggestion of food.

"Take her by her other hand," I tell Rachel, who slides out of the back seat to follow my orders almost before I can voice them.

Together she and I lead Auntie up the steps to the café and guide her through the screen door. Auntie keeps trying to pull away, to go back to the car and see to her dog.

"I've parked in the shade," I plead. "Shellie will be all right for a few minutes."

All the way down Lolo Pass I've been remembering the talk about her low blood sugar, remembering that we did eat a late breakfast in Missoula (but wouldn't her blood sugar be likelier to be lowered by an *early* breakfast?), and telling myself that the first thing to try is to get some sugar into her.

The waitress takes us in at a glance and comes around the counter to help us to a table. She brings a dish of ice cream, and Auntie is persuaded to pick up her spoon and take a tiny bite. Suddenly she seizes her plastic glass of water and darts for the door.

"No, no! You can't take that glass outside! We'll ask for a paper cup of water for Shellie, but first you have to eat that ice cream!"

I drag her back to the table and sit her down. Muttering, she looks for a way around me and finds none. She eats another spoonful of ice cream, and I am aware, on the periphery, of the table of grimy kids in motorcycle regalia, of their averted eyes, and of the silence in the café.

And that is the beginning of the rest of the summer and fall as a series of doctors' appointments. I teach a class, toss my books into my car, and rush across town to pick up my aunt and drive her to the Valley Medical Center. Or to Neuro Diagnostics. Or to Outpatient at the hospital for additional tests.

True, Auntie recovered from her "spell" that afternoon on

Lolo Pass, slipped back from whatever dimension she had wandered into, and was conversing normally in the car by the time we had wound those hundred miles down the river gorge to Lewiston. She has no memory at all of the incident.

"Maybe it was low blood sugar," says Kay, our family practitioner. "But I wish I knew more about these discrete 'spells,' as she calls them. Tell me again about the one in Port Angeles. Apparently it was the first?"

I explain that of course we don't know what might have happened in Port Angeles the morning that she couldn't remember how to cook her breakfast oatmeal. We have only the version of a woman who lived alone for years, no witnesses to her moments.

But lately there was the time when, at two in the morning, my aunt couldn't find her way out of the bathroom, couldn't find the light switch, thought the faucets must be light switches and kept turning them off and on until finally Elizabeth heard the water running and came upstairs to open the bathroom door and let her out.

And there was the Sunday afternoon when, suddenly, she could not speak, but opened and shut her mouth in distress, and then rushed out of the house gobbling and holding her throat. But by the time I had raced up the street in response to Elizabeth's panicky phone call, my aunt was standing under the apricot tree in the back yard with her dog under her arm.

"Auntie? How are you?"

"Fine," she said. "How are you?"

Hearing about it, Kay shakes her head. "It's possible that she had a TIA. A transient ischemic attack." And she explains how the tiny blood clots can clog in one of the carotid arteries, briefly shutting off the blood's supply of oxygen to the brain. ''The clots lodge in the artery very briefly, and then dissolve, and the person is all right again. But sometimes a TIA precedes a real stroke. I think we should do an arteriogram on your aunt to determine whether surgery is warranted to unclog the carotid arteries.''

Then Kay uses a word I have not heard before in my aunt's context. ''Surgery on the carotid artery may reduce her chances of suffering a stroke, but you have to understand it won't alleviate her dementia.''

Dementia. Out of her mind. Rambling the hills of another time and place, trailing shreds of memories with her eyes glazed.

For the first time I realize how far my aunt has set off on her inward journey without me.

4

/ / /

Dementia. *Elizabeth and I talk it over, keeping* our voices low so she won't hear us and come hurrying downstairs, suspicious and surly, to put an end to our tattling. Now we know why Auntie never sews patchwork anymore. She can't keep track of her pieces or her pattern. Now we know why she no longer reads—

"—unless it's a book she's already read a dozen times," Elizabeth points out, "and then she'll open it at random, or just sit and hold it in her lap. She loses her place. Or she can't remember where she started or left off."

"Maybe it *was* a stroke that she had in Port Angeles."

We'll never know. But something certainly happened to Auntie between last November and this summer. I have gone over her fearful phone calls of last winter a hundred times in my own mind, searching after the fact for the moment she began to slip off on her unseen trails.

"She hides it when she forgets," Elizabeth warns. "She'll lie, she'll say anything to cover up her slips."

Elizabeth's voice is tight. I am beginning to worry about her taking a summer class and working ten or twelve hours a day at the veterinary clinic and coming home to cook dinner and cope with Auntie's increasing unpredictability. I am worried about her hostility.

"Auntie's not doing this on purpose," I remind her.

"I *know* that!"

I have to remind myself that this is the first time Elizabeth has encountered the glazed eyes, realized that she is up against irrationality, felt the weight settle on her own shoulders. But if Elizabeth can't handle the situation, what am I going to do? *Your aunt shouldn't be left alone,* Kay has advised me.

And what about Elizabeth?

Told by the dean of the School of Veterinary Medicine at WSU that she should take an additional college course or two and demonstrate to the admissions committee that she can score grades of A, Elizabeth has enrolled in a statistics course at the University of Idaho. Every morning she drives the thirty miles to Moscow, attends her class, drives back to Lewiston, goes to work at the vet clinic, comes home, and cooks dinner for Auntie. Hardly eats, herself. After clearing away, she spreads out her stats homework on the dining-room table. Her notes fill up sheets and sheets of graph paper. Her attention to detail, her exactitude are as relentless as her housekeeping. She sits up all night and studies for quizzes.

"I *know* I did badly! Probably a C. Maybe worse than a C," she moans after a test, and Auntie and I exchange worried looks.

"Was I ever that driven?" I ask Auntie, and she shakes her head.

"Not that I can recall."

The next day, when it turns out that Elizabeth's test was one of the three in the class that scored an A, Auntie and I feel like killing her.

I have worries of my own. Somehow the only time the receptionists at the various clinics seem to want to schedule my aunt's appointments is just before Rachel's violin lesson on Tuesday afternoons. "But that's when Doctor can fit her in," they will sigh, reprovingly, "and she *certainly* should be out by three."

But invariably my aunt's appointments run over—"It will *just* be another minute," insists a nurse, while I chafe; and, sure enough, we miss Rachel's violin lesson again, three times in a row now, and I hear the sanctimonious voices in my head: *If you had any sense at all you'd just forget about those violin lessons, and you'd settle down to what you're supposed to be doing, which is taking care of Auntie—*

What about Rachel?

You never should have had her. Never should have remarried. Look at yourself. Look at Elizabeth. Auntie at least knew herself well enough to stay single.

Then I feel the familiar hot flare of rage, and I choke down the voices—whose voices are they, anyway? Music lessons for Rachel are not my selfish indulgence. Rachel is not my selfish indulgence. I am all Rachel has. And yet my life has gradually become my aunt's. I write the checks to pay her bills, often over her indignant protests, and I balance her checkbook and keep track of her bonds and when they need to be renewed, and her portfolio, and I chauffeur her on her escalating cycle of medical appointments—I listen to her doctors, try to interpret for her, try to be my aunt's memory—

And yet, and yet. I know I'm doing very little when I think about what lies ahead.

But unexpected reinforcement has arrived in the person of Elizabeth's boyfriend, Brian Davies. Brian has been playing pedal steel guitar in a country band on a tour through Switzerland and Germany and has just now got back to Idaho. At first I hardly know what to make of this thin, bearded character. Ski bum, minstrel, where did Elizabeth find him? Playing western swing in the Million Dollar Cowboy Bar in Jackson Hole, Wyoming, she tells me.

"Sure he can live here!" says Auntie. Her eyes light up with something of her old zest. Just let anybody in our family criticize her for letting these two kids live under her roof without benefit of matrimony!

Brian starts working where he can, playing weekend gigs with one or another of the country-and-western bands around town. By day he takes over most of the cooking and laundry, and he checks Auntie's blood sugar every day with an Accu-Test kit, and records its level, and he pulls on leather gloves and forces Shellie's heart medicine down her throat while she struggles and growls and tries to bite him through the gloves.

Also, Brian talks. In the five or six times I ever met Elizabeth's husband, he probably spoke to me a dozen times. *Hello, goodbye, thanks for dinner.* But, then, Dave was a long-sighted elk-hunting boy from west of the mountains who fished with flies like Elizabeth's father, and he was a graduate engineer out of Montana State University. Nobody expects his kind to talk.

Brian and Elizabeth take to dropping by my house on the evenings he isn't playing, to get a break from Auntie and unload her latest follies, or just to visit. When Brian begins to talk about the bands he has opened for and the hopefuls he has played backup for, I gradually relax and pour myself a Jack Daniel's and start keeping Coors in my refrigerator for him.

I've never heard road stories like Brian's. He has been a sideman since his teens, known among musicians for the quality of his work, his ability to improvise, his willingness to drive the bus and set up the sound system, cover for the lead if necessary, and do whatever it takes to get the act on stage. Respected, talented, anonymous, accustomed to the bars and the Legion halls, the bad hours and bad food and booze and dope and hairpin highways of the Rocky Mountain West, he'll never be famous. He's been earning a bare living. And now he's in his late thirties and weary of the life. When Elizabeth started hanging out in the Million Dollar Cowboy Bar, she looked as exotic to him as he did to her.

A ranch girl with a work ethic? She wants to go to veterinary school? Go for it, Brian told her. I'll get a day job, I'll support you.

Looking at these two, I feel a little doubtful, a little envious. How much chance for this softhearted sideman and my driven daughter?

What else I remember about those few autumn weeks before Auntie had her arteriogram: a respite. Brian and Auntie sitting at the kitchen table over coffee, her white head, his shaggy one. He has jerked out the junipers that she hates from under the kitchen window, and he has started a raised bed where she can plant rhododendrons. She can't remember his name. That boy who cooks for me, she calls him. He sure is a fine one. She still can't remember where she left her house key. And the shortened days of fall have thrown off her sense of time. She takes to going to bed earlier and earlier—seven o'clock, six o'clock, as soon as it gets dark. Then, at ten, she gets up again, thinks it's early morning, goes out for the paper, and locks herself out of the house.

Elizabeth in tears. "I feel like it's all my fault, somehow—if only I tried harder—and she blames me, I know she blames me."

"Honey, I don't blame you for anything," says Auntie. She pats Elizabeth on the wrist. "Don't you know the best thing for me would be to drop in my own tracks? If that happens to me, you girls are not to feel sorry."

Auntie, Elizabeth, and me. Our hands clasped. That moment.

Auntie is terrified of having the arteriogram, which she equates with the prospect of having the surgery on her carotid arteries. It is the same surgical procedure that her brother-in-law, my uncle Ervin, underwent last year in Seattle. He suffered a stroke during the surgery; his vision has been damaged, he cannot drive, cannot read or even watch television. The burden of his care has fallen upon eighty-two-year-old Aunt Sylva. We have all been worried about Sylva, we have all felt the isolation of the hundreds of miles we are spread over.

Brian took Auntie to the hospital for her preliminary tests, but he became unnerved when she started to take her clothes off in front of him. So this morning I set my alarm to get her to the hospital by six for the arteriogram. Then I drive home and wake Rachel and get her started for school, read the paper, and go to teach my nine o'clock freshman writing class.

At eleven I have an hour when I can lock my office and drive the few blocks from the campus to the hospital. Auntie is just coming out of the anesthetic, but she's doing fine, she recognizes me, she'll be ready to come home tonight. The nurses load me with instructions for her postoperative care, and I wonder briefly just how Elizabeth, Brian, and I are going to juggle it all.

But when I call at five o'clock, the nurse hesitates. They've moved my aunt to Intensive Care. Yes, I can come over and see her; no, it's very unlikely that she'll be discharged tonight. I will find her pleasantly confused. So I take Rachel with me to the hospital, and she and I find our way through the noise of Intensive Care to the bed where Auntie lies laughing at the ceiling.

"The arteriogram itself went just fine," says the resident. "We don't know quite what's happening now, but we're going to keep her under observation."

Auntie giggles up at him when he steps up to her bedside.

"Do you know these two young ladies?"

"Yes, they're Mary and Rachel!"

"What relation is Mary to you?"

That stumps her. "My aunt by marriage?" she hazards at last, and darts a look at his face to see if she guessed right.

At some point Auntie's "pleasant confusion" boils over into rage.

At three in the morning a fog drifts down from the Palouse to settle along the river and swathe the streets of Lewiston with an eerie indistinction. Driving slowly under the arch of bare branches and the yellowish glow of streetlights, between hedges and parked cars and the glowing eyes of some small crouching animal, I recognize nothing. I might be on any street in any town in Idaho.

Then the sign looms out of the fog, the white H on its blue field, and I get my bearings and turn off this Normal Hill street of shabby duplexes and unrestored Victorians on an avenue lined with the starker architecture of the medical quarter. It is like driving into a future paved with concrete. The office complexes of neurologists and radiologists. The Center for Oncology, windowless as a fort. The glowing sign at the rear entrance of the hospital, where I turn into the empty parking lot.

The phone call in the late evening. Ominously: *Your aunt seems disturbed. We'd like you to talk to her over the phone, try to reassure her—*

The phone call ten minutes ago. *Could you please come down to the hospital and talk to your aunt? She's so belligerent—*

The lights over the parking lot have erased the sky and turned the shadows of shrubs to cutouts. I hear my own footsteps crossing the empty bowl of electric light and concrete. The lobby is quiet. I take the elevator to the fourth floor and hesitate in the dim maze of passages, finally find the arrow to Meds and follow it through double glass doors into a brightly lighted nurses' station where Auntie waits for me, an angry old gnome in a wheelchair.

"Mary? They won't let me leave! I want to get dressed and go home, but they won't let me!"

Her tone is piteous, but her eyes give her away; they swim out of the melted wax of her face, calculating her effect on me, and I have to swallow back my anger at her demands, at the hour, at Rachel left sighing in her sleep at home.

"It's three in the morning, of course they won't let you leave,"

I tell her, and see the fear well up in her eyes. I am on *their* side, against her.

It's been going on all night, starting on the phone.

Mary? They've taken all my money. I need to get out of here and find an attorney and get my money back, but, Mary, they won't let me leave.

No. I won't come and get you. Because it's the middle of the night, that's why. Because the attorneys won't be in their offices until morning. Yes. Yes, first thing in the morning I'll take you to an attorney.

Promise?

How many of my lies will Auntie remember by morning? Where will she be by morning? Earlier this evening I was able to pinpoint her travels, back nearly fifty years to little St. Joseph's Hospital in Lewistown, Montana. She knew she was hospitalized because she had been badly hurt in a mowing-machine accident, that my father's sorrel horses had run away with her and the sickle bar had passed over her foot, nearly severing it at the ankle. She knew she was the most seriously injured patient in the hospital, more critical even than the lineman in the next room, who had nearly been electrocuted on a power pole, and she explained to me how Dr. Solterro had set to work with sutures and saved her foot. But who were all these strange doctors? And where were the Sisters? And my hackles rose with the faint stir of wind, the knowledge that I was in the presence of a consciousness living in 1942.

I don't know how I fit into her time warp, but mine is the only face that is familiar to her. No wonder she is angry and fearful, no wonder she is determined to hang on to me at all costs.

Now she begs, "Mary, will you call Phyllis? Will you ask her to go over and feed my pets?"

"Your pets are all right," I try to reassure her, but she is muttering from somewhere else in her altered geography.

"They won't let me *walk*. How can I get better if they won't let me walk? And I don't even know if my pets are dead or alive."

"Well, you can't walk until morning. You have to wait until the doctor sees you."

"They tied me down, Mary! Hand and foot! I might have had a . . ." She rummages for the lost word. "A—stoppage. A heart stoppage."

Tears roll down her cheeks and course through her wrinkles. I have never seen her cry before, I have to force myself to look. I hate this altered face, like bleached wax, flaccid and sprouted with white whiskers, and I hate the traces of the real Auntie under the ruins, the stubborn jut of her head, her big brown eyes swimming with her claims on me.

All my life I have lived under the same familial injunction that she has: *Never speak of what you feel most deeply.* How can she be breaking the injunction now, manipulating me so shamelessly?

"I don't even know if my pets . . ." Auntie breaks off her complaint and yawns profoundly.

The nurse looms up. "Is Mom ready to go back to bed?"

"She's not my mother, she's my aunt," I correct her, although I know it is useless.

"It's the medication taking effect, once she stopped fighting it. Here we go, honey. Watch your head."

Auntie has lost interest. Her head lolls off the pillow on the wheelchair. She doesn't care about her money or her restraints, or about me. She wants to sleep. Her wattled old chin sags as the nurse wheels her across the corridor to her bed.

"You helped a lot," the nurse says over her shoulder. "We're so glad you came. She tried to bite us."

I watch from the door as she lifts Auntie into bed and guides first one rubbery leg, then the other, between the sheets. I hear the crackle of plastic under Auntie's gown and belatedly realize what it means.

"She isn't continent?"

"Sometimes, after a few days at home, they regain control. But in the morning you'll want to pick up a package of Depends."

"She's being discharged in the morning?"

"Doctor will want to see her first. But probably."

"I don't understand what's happening to her. Was it the arteriogram?"

"Doctor will have to tell you that. Does she seem much changed to you?"

The nurse has tucked the blankets under Auntie's chin as she talked, and now she turns out the light. She is finished, ready to go back to her desk. She is being patient with me.

"Yes, she's changed! I've never seen her like this. The confusion, the belligerence—and can she walk by herself? Can she walk to the bathroom? How can she go home by herself?"

"Well, you can expect some improvement. But, no, she shouldn't be left alone. You'll need to make some arrangements for morning."

It is already morning. Light cannot dawn up here, not here in windowless Meds with its overhead grids of fluorescent lighting, but day stirs in the distant ringing of a telephone, the grind of the elevator and rumble of wheels, the voices in the hall. What should I have done? Been prescient? Hired a relay of home help, starting tomorrow? A phalanx of aides? Which of my morning appointments should I cancel? All?

Time has not stopped. Outside the hospital the lights over the parking lot will be fading out, and the November sun will briefly stain the bricks.

I hardly realize I have spoken. "I don't know if I can do this."

The nurse smiles. She is tired, but her smile is sympathetic. She thinks she knows what troubles me. "Can't you quit your job?"

Auntie has curled herself into the sterile hospital linen, self-absorbed as an infant, already asleep. What has happened to her? Does she dream? Like an infant's, her eyelids are translucent. The rise and fall of her breath barely stirs the white cotton blanket; her shrunken hips barely contour its folds, in sleeping parody of the child I left sleeping alone at home.

5

/ / /

My aunt's friend Phyllis sent me a copy of a short story my aunt wrote four years ago in Phyllis's creative-writing class in Port Angeles:

GRANDSIR
by Imogene Welch

The smell of bacon frying woke me. I crawled out of bed, slid into my jeans and shirt, trotted into the kitchen. Grandsir was sitting at his place sipping his first cup of coffee. From the griddle Ma dished up some hotcakes. I hurried to the wash bench, dipped water, slapped some on my face, took a quick peek at Ma. Her mouth was tight but she was looking at Grandsir, not me. This time of day, my hands weren't what you'd call dirty. I grabbed the towel and gave my face a swipe.

Grandsir passed the plate of cakes my way. He was a lean old man with rusty grey hair. He grinned at me. What had they been arguing about?

"Nope," Grandsir spoke. "I ain't 87, not by a damn sight. I'm 88 if I'm a day." He pointed at Ma with his knife. Ma sniffed. On the table, she dumped her pan of bread dough and punched it down. "Eat up, girl. We got to chop extra wood today. Your Ma is gonna bake."

When we shoved our chairs back, I hurried after Grandsir. I snatched up the chip basket. As Grandsir chopped, I stacked the pieces; then, as I scrabbled around after chips, I thought about age. I was 5, soon old enough to go to school. My brother Ben was 10. It took two numbers to write his age. What could it be like to be 80-something?

"Grandsir, what does it feel like to be in your 80s? Does it hurt?"

"Well," he paused, felt the edge of his blade, spat on his hands and raised the ax again. With a crack, his chunk split. "A feller's stiffer than he used to be. Not so lively. Sometimes you get an ache in a joint, come cold weather. Good thing, stand up slow, be sure you got your feet under you."

Satisfied with the pile of wood at last, Grandsir sunk the ax in his chopping block, stretched and sank down on his restin' chunk to take his breather. From his pocket he pulled a plug of terbaccer. He inspected it closely, giving me a sly look.

"I see you ain't been samplin' my chewin' lately," he said.

My face burned and I ducked my head. Last week I'd seen my chance, gnawed off a good chew and fled behind the barn to try it. I figured I was gonna die before time for dinner. Grandsir found me, held my head through the worst. He didn't tell Ma. For that I was grateful.

Now I flopped down, drew up my knees, watched Grandsir chew. He reminded me some of a cow workin' her cud. He stared at something. A fat bumble bee mumbled above a dandelion blossom. I judged the distance. Too far. He'd never hit it. I bet on the bee.

Grandsir sucked in his cheeks, aimed. Kersplat! The bee and I lost. He hit it fair and square. I stared at the distance, amazed.

"Grandsir, how come you never chop any wood ahead? If you had some extry, you could rest a day, and Grandsir, how long did it take you to learn to spit that far?"

"Girl, one thing I've learned. You want to keep goin', you gotta have something to do. And do it every day. A feller goes down hill quick, you start sittin'.

"Yessir, even spittin'. You got to keep in practice. Remember that, girl."

Auntie's still spitting, for sure. Miraculously, she is on her feet, tottery but determined, when I come to check her out of the hospital in the morning. She wants out of this place, and she doesn't want me out of her sight for fear she might have to stay here ten minutes longer. When the nurse starts to explain her eight or nine prescriptions to me—two of these, three of these, these before meals, these after, these twice a day, but once a day for these—Auntie says, "Yes, yes," dismissively, and snatches them up, cramming them into her purse before I can get an idea what they are. What am I going to do? Who is going to remember all this medication and see that she takes it properly? I can't go so fast, I cannot keep up, I am drowning in my aunt's demands.

Just in time, Brian intervenes. Brian came along this morning to help lift and carry. Though I've gradually come to feel easier with Brian, his presence jitters me almost as badly as Auntie does. I've been on my own too long, I'm not used to assistance. What can Brian possibly think of this crazy old woman? What can he think of me? I'm crying, right in front of him.

To my amazement, Brian puts his arms around me. I fight off the instinct to stiffen and back away. I'm just able to touch my head to the bony unfamiliarity of his shoulder for a moment, to let him hold me.

"Mary, it's going to be all right," he says.

He takes all the prescriptions away from Auntie, spreads them out on the counter at the nurses' station, and studies them.

"Yeah, I know what these are, don't worry. I'll get these figured out."

Auntie and the nurses, too, are a little in awe of Brian. He watches them from under the brim of his cap, beady-eyed and unsmiling, with his hands full of prescriptions, and they back off and allow me to go about the task of signing Auntie out of the hospital at my own pace.

The nurses all assume that Auntie is my mother. I'm used to people jumping to that conclusion, only occasionally bother to correct them. But, they obviously wonder, how is this stern, bearded young man connected to her and me? *Your friend,* one of the nurses finally refers to him, with that certain inflection that makes Elizabeth laugh when I tell her about it.

"Oh, God! Poor Brian!"

A happier time. I am eight months pregnant with Rachel, and Auntie, Elizabeth, and I have gone to shop for a baby crib. Rachel's father is still alive, Brian undreamed-of. At the checkout counter, the three of us laugh and joke until the middle-aged clerk says, "Please, I just have to know. How are you all related to each other?"

My worst lie. Shellie is dead, and I have been afraid to tell Auntie that we had her dog put down while she was hospitalized.

On that night of constant phone calls came a call from Elizabeth. She was in tears. Shellie was worse; her breathing was labored, and she had lost control of her bowels—"and all that white hair, it's all smeared and stuck—oh, Mother, and she tries to bite whenever I go near her—"

"Damn her, if she could just have lasted a few more weeks."

"She's in pain, Mother, and I'm willing to take her down to the vet clinic and have the guys I know do it, but I can't *decide* to do it."

"Then I'll decide. Do it."

What we have learned from the hospital tests is that an old stroke, a stroke so subtle she never knew she suffered it, has damaged Auntie's speech and left a destructive lesion on her brain which continues to eat away at her memory. Was this the stroke she suffered in Port Angeles the morning she could not remember how to cook her breakfast oatmeal? We'll never know.

Furthermore, she suffers from something called seizure syndrome, which accounts for episodes like the one on Lolo Pass earlier this summer. Her carotid arteries are indeed clogged, but her doctor has recommended against the trauma of further surgery. She has prescribed antiseizure medication and an aspirin a day to thin her blood and sent her home. So I have canceled my classes, and now I sit with Auntie in her living room, waiting for Brian to get back from the pharmacy with all her new prescriptions filled.

Auntie can make her intentions known only through curious circumlocutions and hiatuses in her speech, but she is already on her feet before she has been home ten minutes. Wan and hazy as a ghost, she feels her way down the hall and into her bedroom with me hovering anxiously behind her. Does she know where she is? I don't have to ask what she is looking for.

She does ask me, finally, "Did the little boy lie down?"

"Yes," I answer, guessing what she means.

"That was sad."

"Yes."

Inwardly I am boiling with rage I can barely contain. What is it about her and me? Why can't we speak of what we feel? The lesion revealed by the CAT scan will worsen, Kay has told us. It will undermine my aunt's speech, dissolve connectives, and wipe out whole words, never to be rewritten—but even without the lesion, could she and I have talked to each other, except in that encoded language used by women in that remote time and place of her childhood, still in use in my childhood—that baffling, infuriating language, hardly even a spoken language, with its intent always to keep more secrets than it revealed?

I won't get better? Auntie asked her doctor, point-blank.

Kay chose her words, met Auntie's eyes. *You'll have good days and bad days,* she answered. *But no. You won't get better.*

But Auntie's still spitting. When I broach the idea of a companion, she is adamant. "No. It wouldn't be convenient. I don't want anybody else in the house."

Then, seeing that I am going right ahead and phoning names from the list I got from the hospital, she turns pathetic. Fixes me with those big brown eyes, turns her melted-wax face up to mine. "I don't *need* anybody, Mary. Can't you see how well I'm doing? I know you'd tell me if I weren't."

"But the doctor has told us you shouldn't be alone."

"But I have Elizabeth downstairs, and that boy who cooks for me. Why do I need anybody else?"

"Because Elizabeth has a job. She's out of the house all day. And there are things that Brian can't do for you. Bathe you, for example, and change your Depends. Besides, Brian's looking for a job."

Unspoken between us is the knowledge that I could solve her dilemma. I could take care of Auntie and help her to pretend that she is taking care of herself. I'd have to give up teaching. I'd have to move into her house with her—mine has too many stairs, and anyway she'd never stand for moving out of her own house. I'd rent mine out, I suppose. Or sell it.

Fragments of conversations over the past months rearrange themselves:

"There are ways," says my friend Kim. "My parents moved a trailer back of my grandma's house and lived in it themselves. They were able to keep her at home for another two years. Then they advertised and hired women to stay with her in shifts, around the clock, for another year. They were always able to find women who wanted to get away from their husbands for a few days a week."

"I don't think she's as bad off as you make her sound," my mother argues over the long-distance line. "She's always taken her bath and put her dirty clothes back on, always done things like that. She'll learn not to lock herself out of her house if she does it often enough. You're just making too much of it."

"I worry about the river," says my sister. "How far—three blocks away?"

"Have you read this book on the care of Alzheimer's sufferers?"

asks Kay, when I turn to her. "It's called *The Thirty-six Hour Day,* and it'll give you an idea of what you're headed for."

It does.

The sanctimonious voices. *What you really should have done, Mary, was to move out to Port Angeles to live with her. In her old familiar surroundings, in her own house and garden, you could have kept her alert and happy for a long time. Remember, she invited you to move in with her long ago. Pointed out that you could get a teaching job in Port Angeles, that the two of you could share expenses, save money—but no, you felt smothered even then. You had to go your own way. And now— now, when you could make your life hers—*

Instead, I hire Julie.

Julie is a pale sad-faced girl, diabetic and vastly overweight. She is a licensed home caregiver. Her tasks are to supervise Auntie's bath and watch that she doesn't fall, make sure she puts on clean clothes, eats her breakfast, and takes her various medications according to the meticulous chart Brian has drawn up and posted on the door of the refrigerator. Julie will take a walk with Auntie every morning, come home and fix coffee for her and read the newspaper to her, keep her company, and fix her lunch, all for $5.85 an hour.

Auntie hates Julie on sight.

It is true that, in many respects, Auntie is more than Julie's match. For instance, tough old Auntie has walked a mile every morning of her life for years. Now, when Julie goes with her, Auntie sets an evil pace and walks poor panting Julie right into the ground.

It is also true that Julie's values are not Auntie's. "Spend money! Spend money!" Auntie hisses. "That's all she knows to do! She told me how a friend of hers got a support check from her husband and they went right out and *spent* it!"

Poor gentle Julie, ours is surely the first family she has worked for that has not owned a television set. At loose ends, snubbed by Auntie, she talks to her friends on the telephone and nibbles constantly, until Elizabeth complains, "I can't keep groceries in the house! Crackers, cookies, chips—Julie inhales them!"

Elizabeth is tense, panicky. For months her perfectionism has been warning her that the deterioration of the household is her own personal fault. Now she has had enough. She wants to move out. "It's spooky, Mother. Auntie gets up and roams at night. I woke up last night, and there she was, standing beside my bed and staring down at me."

Brian, more resilient, gets out of bed and chases Auntie back upstairs and into her own bedroom, tells her to stay there until morning. Sometimes she does, sometimes she doesn't. There is a word, I learn from Kay, for this roaming about in the middle of the night: *sundowning.*

"Can't you keep her from going to bed until a little later in the evening?" Kay suggests. "Until ten o'clock, at least?"

"Not a chance. She goes to bed with the chickens. Six o'clock, five o'clock, now that it's getting dark so early."

"No wonder she can't sleep all night."

How can Brian stand it here? Why doesn't he just leave, and take Elizabeth with him? Months later Elizabeth and I speculate that it was his years as a sideman. Maybe, compared with keeping a country-western band on the road, taking care of Auntie seemed tame. ("No," says Brian, "I just wanted to be part of your family. I didn't want to go on waking up alone in a motel room for the rest of my life.")

I believe that Auntie is in love with Brian. No, don't laugh at this old woman, this stringy bag of bones and gristle, blear-eyed and messy and confused. Her face quivers with wattles, her shoulder blades jut out, her breasts hang somewhere in the neighborhood of her waist. But I've watched her mood lift when Brian walks into the room, seen her sparkle at him, seen her tender glance when he isn't looking. Only Brian can coax her out of her sulks, get her to cooperate with Julie and take her bath, get her to laugh.

Elizabeth thinks that Auntie hates her, and I have observed her increasing surliness with Elizabeth, her mean jabs and little asides. What does Auntie think? That, perhaps, she can run off Elizabeth and keep Brian?

But I'm not laughing at this old woman, who, even through the haze of her dementia, longs for just what I secretly long for: to love and be loved. When Auntie's eyes soften and her lips move in an unconscious smile, I know—think I know—that she has drifted into the luxury of fantasy.

But her fog is worsening. Some days she is reduced to mumbling. The meal she is eating, the location of her own bed fade out of her memory. Sometimes she cannot remember that she had started to get dressed. Early one morning Elizabeth looks up from the breakfast she is cooking and is startled to see Auntie, clad in nothing but her undershirt, watching her from the kitchen door.

"Auntie! Go put your clothes on!"

"Whah?"

To keep her from straying outdoors, naked and disoriented, I come up with the idea of equipping the doorknobs with those plastic caps meant to thwart toddlers. Auntie, who has promised us solemnly not to try to go walking without a companion, darts for the front door the minute she sees her chance, runs up against the plastic cap on the knob, and weeps in frustration.

"They ought to be ashamed. To lock in an old lady. There might be a fire, and I might be—might be—might be—" She cannot find the word she needs, she weeps afresh. "Oh, what did I ever do to deserve this?"

Advice abounds.

Dear Ann Landers:

I'm sick and tired of hearing from these bums who put their parents in nursing homes and then complain that they don't recognize them, so what's the point of visiting them? And what about the expense, they whine? Excuses, excuses, etc., etc. Well, I just want the bums to know that Mama is 101, and she hasn't recognized anybody in the family in ten years, and that's *just fine*. And her care is using up all our money, and we won't be able to send our kids to college when the time comes, and that's *just fine*. When God wants Mama, he'll take her.

(Signed) Doing the Right Thing in Grangeville

When I try to explain the shambles of my semester to the dean, he remarks, "I wouldn't put a dog in a nursing home," and I feel like killing him.

"Mother insisted on going to a nursing home," says my friend Shirley. "That was her great gift to us."

And I feel the familiar surge of anger: is my life in Auntie's hands to bestow as a gift or to withhold?

Reading *The Thirty-six Hour Day* sends me to the self-help books in the public library. In these personal narratives I find plenty of folks who have coped willingly, gladly, for years. Sometimes with almost a competitive edge. Here's a man, for example, who gave up his career and his girlfriend to keep his father out of a nursing home. None of the other sons would help. But, oh, it can be done, he says, it can be done. He tots up his thousands of dollars in lost salary, details the degradation of tending his father's body. But he does think you can go too far. He draws the line at the friend who picked his father's feces out of his bowels by hand and points out that there are good stool-softeners on the market.

The problem Auntie and I have got here is me.

I have never been worth a good goddamn at self-sacrifice. Never. I'm the girl who got married at eighteen so I wouldn't have to go back to the ranch. Then I refused to go to work to put my first husband through college, went to college right along with him on money borrowed from my grandmother, even though it nearly killed his parents—*You're willing to trample on anybody to get where you're going,* hurtles the accusation after me through the years. *You're hard as nails! You're selfish! Selfish!*

You're goddamn right I am. I may hear sanctimonious voices in my head, but I parked my first two babies with sitters, dragged them as toddlers behind me through a Ph.D. program, taught them to fold laundry at the same time I taught them to read, withstood all the pressures and advice and popular wisdom of the day. *Stay at home with your babies. Don't threaten your husband's ego.* And now, after all these years of resisting the voices, here I am in Idaho, in my safe, private space, with the work that is my lifeline and my last child to raise, and I finally understand the truly murderous rage with which Virginia Woolf throttled the angel in the house. For Auntie and I are locked in mortal combat for our lives.

Enter into the pretense that I am fine. I am fine because I have you to cover for me, rescue me, take care of me, and pretend that I am taking care of myself.

What about the Riverside Gardens?

A pleasant place, not a nursing home at all, but a residential center. Moderately expensive—but Auntie can afford its fees, for her lifetime habit of thriftiness has provided her with a substantial cushion of investments. And Riverside offers varying levels of care designed to allow its residents as much independence as they can manage; some live in apartments with kitchenettes and drive their own cars, others require considerable assistance from a trained staff. The hostess takes me on a tour of the carpeted corridors, the day room, the elegant dining room, the straw flowers and mirrors and Renoir prints. She shows me the menus. The private rooms. The wide-screen TV.

Auntie will have none of it.

"If you make me go and live in that place, I'll have nothing to do for the rest of my life but sit in a corner and cry!"

When I drive her across the river and check her in for a trial weekend, Auntie weeps all the way. "Oh dear! Oh dear! I can't bear it, I can't bear it!"

When did she learn how to be so manipulative? I wonder on the way home. It seems so completely out of character for Auntie, and yet she plucks all my emotional strings like a virtuosa born to the tune. Poor old lady, poor pitiful old lady. That her predicament really seems pitiable to me doesn't make me feel any better; the worst part is that she retains just enough of her wits to realize she is losing them.

And what has Auntie's life to do, after all, with the tasteful floral wallpapers and thick carpets of the Riverside Gardens? Child of the homestead frontier, proud of her austerity, her ability to make do, she has always despised interior decoration as wasteful, and luxury and even comfort as debilitating. Television, bingo, the special seniors' version of Trivial Pursuit—with what contempt she dismisses these activities! The company of the other residents —she shrugs, indifferent. Far better to enjoy her own solitary resources than to put up with bores. But what are her resources, now that she can neither read nor write, nor quilt nor dig in a garden?

When I go back to get her on Sunday afternoon, she hobbles up eagerly, lifts her swimming eyes to mine—"I was so afraid you would never come for me!" And when I seem unmoved by her pathos, she turns venomous. "Slop!" she flings at me when I make the mistake of asking what she had for dinner.

But Elizabeth, Brian, and I have enjoyed a wonderful restful weekend. No night rambles, no accidents, no confrontations with Auntie or desperate phone calls. Even Julie got to go home to her relatives and her soaps.

"And, you know, your aunt was just fine all the time she was

here with us," the Riverside hostess assures me. "That's so often
how it is, you know. They complain to their families, but soon
they come to think of us as home, and they're eager to get back
to us when they've been away for a visit."

With weekends to ourselves, we may just be able to gird up
and continue caring for her at home during the week. So—over
Auntie's pleas, over her threats and muttered invective—we try
again. The next Friday, I drive Auntie across the bridge, just as
the streetlights on the Clarkston side of the river are beginning to
loom in the leaden late afternoon, and check her into Riverside
Gardens in time for dinner.

But while we've been laying our plans in whispered conferences
in the kitchen, Auntie apparently has been laying hers. She has
told us she *will not* stay in that place again, and she means it.

The first phone call from Riverside Gardens comes at ten
o'clock that night, just as I have drawn a long breath and poured
my single whiskey. My aunt has run away, the staff have no idea
where. I glance out the window as I grab a jacket and my car
keys; it's about zero tonight, and snowing lightly. Before I can get
out the door, the phone rings again. They've found her, or at least
the police have. One of the squad cars picked her up a block or
two from Riverside, hiking along in her nightgown and bare feet.

"We're going to send her over to the hospital by ambulance
for examination," the night nurse explains over the phone. "And
her doctor has ordered a sedative."

By the time I can drive across the river and race up to the
nurses' station on the second floor, my aunt is drowsy with medication and doesn't know me. *Now what do we do,* I wonder, while
the Riverside night nurse explains that apparently my aunt escaped
through a first-floor window. She could have been dead from ex-

posure on a night like this. And what if she'd headed for the river? What if she tries a second-floor window next time?

"We don't lock our doors and windows from the inside," explains the nurse. "We're not really that kind of facility."

We'll see how she seems in the morning, we finally decide, and I drive home through the thickening snow and the wan flicker of the first Christmas lights swaying in the faint wind from the river. Can it really be just six months since Elizabeth and I moved Auntie out of Port Angeles? What to do, what to do? Elizabeth can't, won't go on. Brian has been a solid rock of support, but how much more can I ask of him? That leaves me. I am remembering the words of a friend in Montana who nursed her bedridden grandmother at home for seven or eight years—*I could do it because she was bedridden. When they're mobile, one person can't do it. They can run off while you're going to the bathroom.*

First word in the morning is that my aunt seems calm, that she seems not to remember her errantry of last night. But in the late afternoon the day nurse calls again, beside herself.

"Can you get over here, quick? Your aunt's gone on a rampage."

The hostess stands behind her desk, wringing her hands, when I race through the lobby with Rachel racing after me like the tail on a kite. "I'm so sorry, I'm so sorry," her lament fades after us.

The nurse, when we find her, blooms with rage. "We can't keep her here! We're waiting for the ambulance right now, we'll get her over to the hospital and get her sedated, but we can't take her back. She needs nursing-home care. We're not geared for violent clients."

Violent?

Well, she's torn down the Christmas decorations in the day room, smashed the ornaments off the tree, ripped down the curtains from the windows, slugged the aide who tried to stop her, kicked and bitten—

With my head ringing, I walk down the corridor to the nurses' station where my aunt waits, grinning to herself, in a straight-backed chair.

Rachel glances at me, tucks herself back against a wall.

"She's had a pill," whispers an aide who is keeping a nervous surveillance.

"Auntie?"

She barely glances at me. Her eyes glint with ferocious reminiscence. "I got in some real good licks," she says, savoring, and all of a sudden I want to wring her neck.

"What's the matter with you? Do you know how many times I've had to run back and forth across that bridge—and they won't *let* you stay here now, I don't know what we'll do—and then you brag how you hit people. Don't you know those aides can't hit you back? I'm ashamed of you!"

"Good!" she says. "Good! I'm glad somebody in the family is ashamed of me."

The ambulance has arrived. And I can hear the bustle in the corridor, the whispers, the legend in the making—*Did you see her? Did you see the mess she made? Those broken ornaments? Maybe she's crazy. Maybe she's possessed. All of a sudden she just hauled off and hit that aide in the stomach. Did you see it?*

"Imogene again, eh?" says the EMT. Apparently he's the one who transported her to the hospital last time. He shakes his head. She doesn't look dangerous. The pill has taken hold, and she has turned into a little white-haired gnome, nodding off in her chair. The EMT loads her on a gurney and wheels her out. The next time I see my aunt, she will be so heavily tranquilized that she will seem catatonic.

I'm ashamed of you!

Good! I'm glad somebody in the family is ashamed of me.

For weeks to come I think that those may be the last rational words my aunt and I ever speak to each other.

6

/ / /

The Valley Villa is a rambling structure in the Lewiston Orchards, which is a self-contained neighborhood on the plateau above the town of Lewiston proper, threaded by narrow potholed streets and interrupted by pastures where, in the winter, horses nuzzle the frozen grass. The sky is crosshatched by the darkened branches of maples and locust trees on days so gray and slow that I would hardly believe in a world beyond the crumbling pavement if I could not see, from the Villa's parking lot, the whitened tips of the Rockies to the east and the Blue Mountains of Oregon to the southwest.

The Villa has a locked wing for Alzheimer's and other badly confused patients. You turn left through the lobby, go past the business office, and enter the door to the north wing by pushing a red button. You get out again by tapping a secret numerical code on a pad set high on the wall. They have to keep changing the code, because some of the patients still retain enough wits to hang around and memorize the sequence of numbers as visitors tap them out.

"Mom, is Auntie going to live in the Villa Villekula?" asks Rachel, who has been reading *Pippi Longstocking,* and I can't help laughing at the association. The name will become a part of our family's private language: *I have to run up to the Villa Villekula this afternoon to see Auntie.*

"If her violence continues, we can't keep her, and the next step will be the state mental hospital in Orofino," the director of nursing tells Elizabeth and me that first afternoon. "But we have an empty bed in the locked wing, and we'll give your aunt a try. We can supervise her medication more carefully than they could at Riverside, and we'll get her down to the minimum level. We don't believe in heavy tranquilization here."

She shows us around the facility. The corridors are linoleum here, and the heavy odor of disinfectant hangs in the air. No Renoir prints here, no fresh flowers. This is a place battened down for a last stand, where pale cadavers gaze from their beds or hunch over aluminum walkers in the halls. Staffers in white uniforms with black security belts hurry back and forth, pausing to pat a liver-spotted hand or kiss a cheek.

At the locked door Elizabeth claps her hand over her mouth and runs, white-faced, back down the hall and through the lobby toward the glass doors.

The director makes no comment. Without even pausing in her patter of explanation, she guides me into the north wing, shows me bathrooms, bedrooms, nurses' station, activities room, all scrupulously clean. Ancient humans sit or stand around, vacant-eyed, and the director greets them by name. Some answer, some stare, some hardly react.

The dining room—the activities director—the newsletter—

And then she takes me back to the business office to sign a myriad of forms.

No, I explain all over again. My aunt is Miss Welch, not Mrs. Welch. She never married, never had children. I am not her daughter, I am her niece. I am the one she turned to when she could not take care of herself. No—no other relatives closer than Seattle. No one but me to notify. Yes, I have her power of attorney.

No, I won't assume financial responsibility for her. Yes, she has enough income, between her pension and her Social Security check and her dividends, to pay for her nursing-home care.

"That is so rare," says the director, finishing with another form, and I remember all the penny-pinching, all the years of austerity.

Her level of education? She has a bachelor's degree, she was a teacher.

Close friends?

"I have their addresses, I'll keep in touch," I promise, thinking about Phyllis and her family back in Port Angeles. Later I wonder: Was she inquiring about a *significant other?*

But, no, never ever, so far as I knew.

Finally the director asks, "How do you feel about signing a no-resuscitation order?"

I sign.

Half an hour later, when I go out to the car, Elizabeth is waiting for me, white and tearful. "I couldn't help it. I couldn't stand it in there."

"I know."

"I just keep thinking, If only I'd done more, if I were a better person, I could have kept this from happening to her. Oh, Mother—"

The winter sun bounces off the cement and strikes the car windows with red dazzles. I feel blinded, stunned, as though my skull has been turned inside out and my own inner voices have been emptied out of sick dark echo-chambers and exposed to broad daylight.

I lean across the seat and, for the first time since her childhood, I manage to embrace my older daughter.

Gradually they drain the sedatives out of my aunt's system. Over weeks she rouses, ceases her compulsive shuffling of her hands and feet. Raises her head, recognizes me. Speaks words again.

The director thinks that my aunt is a good candidate for physical therapy, that she can be massaged and exercised out of her wheelchair and on her feet again. Will I sign the necessary papers to permit the therapy?

Sure I will.

And the next week I get a frantic phone call: my aunt's first act, on regaining her mobility, has been to climb up on her bed, somehow push the screen off the window, squirm through it, and lower herself down six feet to the ground. She was trotting off into the unknown when a neighbor looked up from spading his early garden and hurried to head her off.

And so this afternoon, in the late summer of 1991, when I press the red button that opens the locked door to the north wing of the Villa Villekula, the first sight I see at the far end of the corridor is the knot of consternation around the nurses' station with my aunt at its center. She is arguing, wringing her hands, shaking her white head in distress.

Three staffers see me and point simultaneously down the hall: "Look, look! There's Mary! Mary's coming to see you!"

"Oh, boo hoo hoo," sobs my aunt. "I can't stand it, I can't stand it."

"She thinks the ice cream hasn't been paid for," explains one of the aides.

"It's been like this all day," says another, wearily.

A dozen old men and women are standing or sitting around, spooning up the last of their ice cream or, in one or two cases, lolling back in their wheelchairs and having their ice cream spooned into their mouths for them. Some seem oblivious or indifferent to my aunt's distress, while others look on with the frank interest of children. I recognize the woman with the iron-gray bobbed hair who often tries to take her clothes off, the shriveled little woman who wants my purse, the robust old fellow who crawls around behind furniture and eavesdrops.

"They'll think I don't know how to manage money," my aunt laments. "But it was too much to ask. I couldn't, couldn't, couldn't—oh, now I can't think of my word. Oh, I feel so useless, I feel so useless."

"I brought you a letter," I offer as a distraction.

She accepts the envelope from me, fumbles ineffectually at the sealed flap with her thumb, and dissolves into a fresh torrent of tears.

"Oh, oh, oh! None of them paid me for the ice cream, none of them!"

I gather what happened is that the aides asked her to help pass out the ice cream for the afternoon treat. Though my aunt resists the therapy games and social hours, sometimes she likes being assigned small tasks, setting the tables or folding laundry, that she can see some purpose to. But not today. Her hands are as soft and puffy as though they have been soaked in water, and her face looks like a sponge for tears.

Last week Kay prescribed an antidepressant, which turned off my aunt's tears for a few days, but now the effect seems to have worn off. No wonder the staffers are hurrying around on their various tasks and avoiding my eye. They probably hope I'll stay and distract her for the rest of the afternoon.

"Shall I read your letter to you?"

She hands it over, weeping, while I look for a place for us to sit. Although an aide seems constantly to be mopping the linoleum floor of the day room and sponging the plastic-covered seats of the chairs, it's a good idea to be careful where you walk or sit. I avert my eyes as a gaunt old fellow in a wheelchair glares at me, works his mouth, and expectorates his loose gob on the floor between his feet.

Sitting with my back carefully turned toward the old gobber, I open my aunt's letter and read it aloud to her.

It is from Aunt Sylva. *I went on an outing with the senior citizens to Mount Rainier, and it was lovely. Do you remember when you and I took Mother to see Mount Rainier, years ago? I think Mother enjoyed that trip.*

A deeply wrinkled woman with eyes as dark and bottomless as a deer's sits down beside my aunt and studies her face. Then she looks at me. "Blah, blah, blah, blah, blah!" she shouts.

"Oh, boo hoo hoo! I can't remember a trip. I can't even write a letter back to Sylva." Another thought strikes her. "Is Ervin still alive?"

"No. Don't you remember that I told you? Ervin died last May."

"Blah, blah, blah, blah, blah! Blah, blah, blah, blah, blah!"

I don't know what else to do, so I sit quietly and listen to my aunt's sobs. I would hug a crying child. But although my aunt's dementia is gradually erasing her memories, beginning with the most recent and eroding its way back through time; although she cannot concentrate, cannot remember how to feed herself except by reflex; although much of her deterioration seems a progress in reverse through the stages of childhood, much still resists this analogy. She is not a child and she will not be treated as a child. And yet, who is she, these days?

On impulse, to distract her, I ask, "Auntie, do you remember anything about a woman named Irene Bartok?"

My aunt's reaction to that name is amazing. Her tears vanish, her features reassemble, and her voice, when she answers, almost sounds like herself.

"Oh, yes. Her."

"Did you know her?"

I know that the answer to my question is yes, because for a while I was doing research into Montana ranch life in the 1930s, with the idea of writing a novel, and all the old people I interviewed wanted to tell me Irene Bartok's story. I know that Irene, like my aunt and my mother and father, was one of the Montana-born children on the homestead frontier in Fergus County, and that she was popularly supposed to have killed her husband, in about 1935, and gotten away with it.

"How old was Irene when you knew her?"

"Seventeen," says my aunt, definitely. "She was a big strong girl. Wore her hair—'' One old hand makes a chopping gesture at ear level. A bob. ''And the gossip was that she was a, was a—''

The blah-blah woman is listening intently.

''Prostitute?''

My aunt nods. ''They said that because she lived over the— can't think—place where they kept horses—''

''She lived over the livery stable? In Denton?''

A nod.

''You knew something about the murder,'' I prompt her, ''because someone you knew met Irene and her mother out on the prairie alone one night.''

My aunt nods again. ''I was going out with, with—'' And she actually laughs at herself. ''Never thought I'd forget that name.''

But I remember it.

And with the knowledge stirs the thin shiver of recognition. I feel the shock of the link falling into the chain.

''Was it Ludwig?''

''Ludwig,'' she repeats, correcting my pronunciation. *Lew-doh-vig.* ''It's the Bohemian for *Lewis.* He liked to dance, and we used to go to dances.''

But it is Irene Bartok's story that has caught my aunt's attention today, and together she and I tell it to each other. How half the countryside had seen Irene in the early evening with her husband at a dance at some remote country school. How, much later that night—the custom in those days was to pause for supper at midnight, then go on dancing until three or four o'clock in the morning—as he was riding home by a shortcut, Ludwig met Irene and her mother out on the prairie, miles from anywhere. Irene's husband was not with them, nor was he ever seen again. Did his bones bleach in some nameless crevice?

Leaning over to listen, the blah-blah woman nods as profoundly as though the story confirms her own deepest suspicions.

"I can't remember any more," says my aunt. But she is calm now, if tremulous, and the blank bewilderment in her eyes is gone. She nods to herself as though she is listening inwardly to a damaged transmission. I am struck all over again by the power of story, the lifeline of narrative that links us across the generations.

But the point of this story—the old unforgiving homestead code against sexual transgression, the savage impulses between men and women, the acting out of their worst fears—what does it mean to my aunt?

And what about Ludwig? His is the story I really want to know.

"Maybe you can remember more about Lud to tell me next time," I suggest, and my aunt smiles in her reverie. I think I know what she sees inwardly, and my heart twists, because by this time Elizabeth and I have found the snapshot she kept of Lud, and I know that he was a big-shouldered young man with a grin that flashed under the shadow of a cowboy hat, and I know—think I know—at least a part of his story and my aunt's.

Sooner or later, they tell me, my aunt will not recognize me. But today she rouses herself and walks me to the door at the end of the corridor. She watches as I tap out the code that will unlock the door, but she does not try to slip out with me as she used to do.

"I'll see you next week," I promise.

And she nods.

Outside is a blaze of late-afternoon sun, softening asphalt, and sycamore leaves hanging under the promise of fall heat to come in Lewiston, Idaho. I can hear the soft swish of sprinklers across lawns and the rumble of unhurried traffic on Burrell Avenue, and I can see the mountains to the east and to the southwest like the barely revealed rim of a giant blue bowl. It all looks real, and I feel as far from that sick corridor of disinfectants and damaged wits as I do from the Montana prairie of 1935, when a young man met a girl and her mother in the false dawn and believed that he had met two murderers.

I possess more of my aunt's repository of memories than she does, nowadays, though I don't understand all the connections. The thread of narrative attaches itself, spun thin, endless, stretching across the parking lot and the street as I drive away from the Villa Villekula. It will stretch as far as I will ever go. In a sense, I am possessed. My life is hers, after all.

7

/ / /

So, Imogene, where shall you and I walk together, and what questions shall we ask? Do we want to know why we both ended up alone, behind the barricades of our own walls and silences and the illusion of safe terrain? What we ran from, and where we failed each other? Whether there's any hope for me, and whose name I might try to remember in my dotage?

Over in Montana is a certain place, a deep cleft in the bluffs where a creek has dug its measureless contortions into the shadows of hills on its way to the Judith River. Sometimes the creek widens, and in summer it sparkles over its gravel bars, and in winter it hides its miles of bends under a cloud of steam rising from its warm springs. To find this place is to know the gravel road that splits off from the highway between Lewistown and Denton, climbs through wheat fields, and then drops down into the cleft. Down here it gets dark early.

Imogene? Are you listening? Are you with me as I go back to the beginning?

Sometime around 1897 a man named Joe Dancey built a cabin of cottonwood logs on the high slope above the Judith River breaks. Pines clung by their roots in the gorges and dripped resin in the heat, but sagebrush grew waist-high up on the slope, and sandstone broke through the thin topsoil, and nothing sheltered Dancey's flimsy cabin from the wind or shaded it from the sun, which in summer burned the shale and set mirages dancing through the bunchgrass. Dancey didn't mind the heat. The high country always cooled off at night, even in July and August. Dancey slept alone in his clothes and rode his saddle horse down the trail in the mornings to work for Theo Hogeland, who had started to grub the underbrush out of his bottomland on Warm Spring Creek.

Brush grew so thick along the creek, Uncle Theo said later, that a man couldn't crawl through it. Chopping it out was a hot and dirty job. The air stayed still and thick down there, and branches snapped back from the ax and whipped across the men's faces with brittle stubs and thorns that seemed to aim for their eyes. Uncle Theo and Dancey hooked onto the roots with a chain and a team of workhorses and strained until the horses dripped with sweat and lathered under the harness and along their privates. The men worked grimy and itching and festooned with beads of blood along their scratches, and they slapped at mosquitoes and breathed gnats into their mouths and noses. As they grubbed out the brush, they stacked it in loose pyres to dry and burn.

Of course, Joe Dancey was hardly more than a boy back then, but he sweated right alongside of Uncle Theo until sixty acres of creek bottom was bare dirt heaved up and cratered and stacked with a grotesque harvest of brush piles. However, Dancey was odd even then. He always liked to head for home around sundown, which came early on the creek bottom. He didn't like the dark, and he didn't like cold weather, either. When the storms of the equinox brought the first light snowfall and Uncle Theo thought it was safe to begin burning his brush piles, Dancey was gone, nobody knew where.

Over the years Uncle Theo eventually got used to Dancey's leaving without a word and showing up again in the spring. Still, that first time Dancey disappeared, Theo must have felt a little uneasy. It wasn't so common at that time in Montana for a white man to drop out of sight. Each of the few settlers along the Judith River knew who the others were and where the others were. The Samples at the river crossing, the Pernots at the foot of the South Moccasin Mountains, the Barneys, and the Hogeland brothers— Abe at the mouth of the Little Judith and Theo himself on his creek bottom—Theo knew them all, and all were accounted for.

He would have taken the time one afternoon to ride up the trail to Dancey's place, but he found the corral empty, no saddle under the lean-to, no tracks in the blown snow. It was a sorry spread, hardly better than an old badger's diggings, a sod-roofed cabin without even windows, nothing about it to look as though Dancey intended it to more than tide him over from one summer to the next. It looked like a regular breed's nest, and Theo thought it might be true that there was some Indian in Dancey, that he was one of the breeds that had come down from the Milk River country to settle on Big Spring Creek. It would explain Dancey's shiftlessness.

But Theo's mind was relieved. If Dancey had broken his neck somewhere, his horse at least would have come home.

Theo had better things to think about than Joe Dancey's where-abouts. He had followed his brother Abe out from staid Bucks County, Pennsylvania, to the empty, unsettled spaces of Montana to file a homestead claim, and he had had a reason for picking this hole at the base of the creek bluffs for his place. The sun might set early, and the wagon road might teeter down a precarious grade, but down here were the warm springs in the creek, which held off the worst of the thirty-below-zero Montana winters. Down here was shelter for the stock, and a growing season long enough for fruit to ripen. Theo looked ahead and saw more than his brush barn and the tiny house he had built out of sawed lumber. As soon as the ground thawed in the spring he would harrow his sixty cleared acres and set out his apple trees. And plums. And gooseberries. Theo planned to make the wilderness bloom.

By the spring of 1905 his saplings were already setting on fruit. But Theo imagined graciousness and comfort and sprigs grown into shade trees over his lawn. One of the last things he did before he left for Pennsylvania in June of that year was to hitch his horses to the wagon and drive up his hairpin road and down the bluffs on the other side until he reached the river, where cottonwoods grew in lofty groves and strewed their drifting cotton across the hazy willows and into the current. Theo dug up a cottonwood sprout and packed its roots in a wet gunny sack for the ride home in the wagon. He planted it, a gray wand with a dozen leaves, by the wire gate in front of the house.

When he returned to Montana a few weeks later with the for-mer Miss Emma Finney at his side, Theo was pleased that his cottonwood sprout was flourishing, but just to be on the safe side he drove an ax handle into the sod and tied up the sprout, so his brother's smaller children wouldn't trample it when Abe and his family drove over in the wagon to meet Em and help celebrate the Fourth of July.

More than twenty years earlier, Abe's wife had left a fourteen-room house in Pennsylvania to travel with the first of her babies by train and then by stagecoach across all the miles of sparser and sparser settlement, the badlands and river breaks and prairie of what was still the Montana Territory, until at last she came to Fergus County and the cabin Abe had built for her on a sage slope. Now she had seven more children, all born in Montana, and her face and hands were honed thin and tight.

When she saw her new sister-in-law looking through a pair of thick round spectacles at the trampled bunchgrass and barbed-wire fence around the house, she thought that Em at least would have neighbors and a house and garden and fresh milk from the start, though down here in the cleft, with nothing to see but a wagon road leading across the creek and up the slope to the crippled pines and the sandstone rims and the sky, she might not appreciate her advantages.

But Em was already making plans.

"My furniture's coming," she explained to her sister-in-law. She stood sturdily, her eyes gleaming behind her spectacles. "Theo is going to build onto the kitchen, so we can move out the cream separator and the milking things to make room for my dining-room table. It stretches out to seat twenty."

For Em, as for her husband, Montana was raw material. They had left Bucks County, Pennsylvania, only to replicate it.

/ / /

Now, in the last years of the twentieth century, these hills and creek bottoms still are tinged with green in the spring from the rains. Balsamroot colors the upper hillsides yellow. Wild roses bloom all through June along the highway from Lewistown, and sweet clover grows rank and heavy in the borrow pits. When summer digs in, the rains stop and the weeds toughen up.

The North and South Moccasins, the Snowies, the Judiths— these are the low mountains which hem in central Montana, the familiar blue rims of my childhood and Imogene's childhood. She was born in 1910, in Great Falls, and a few weeks later the same buttes and slice of slow daylight moon would have followed the wagon that carried her home to the three hundred and twenty dryland acres that her mother and father had claimed on the slope above the Judith River breaks. She came to awareness on the homestead, knowing nothing of history.

Imogene would not have known until she learned it from books that she had grown up on what had been hunting grounds for the Blackfeet and the Crow. She couldn't have known about the wide trail the Nez Percés had cut across central Montana when they fled ahead of General Howard in 1877, or about the wagon ruts left by the half-breeds in the same year. However, Uncle Theo and Aunt Em she knew as elderly neighbors whose nephew her younger sister one day would marry.

Theo Hogeland had come to this place and seen that the fall grass was tawny and rich, and he dreamed of raising sheep, a thousand or more head of his own. He imagined grainfields. And good roads and schools. *We have teenagers in the neighborhood who can't read!* he exclaimed, and he pressed his brother, Abe, into service as the first teacher at the school by the dipping tank.

For his part, what Theo could not have imagined were the great shifts following World War II, and the changes in agricultural economy and technology that caused the rural population to fade slowly from the farms and ranches that had been so dearly won and held for so few years during the drought-stricken 1920s and the devastation of the 1930s. He could not have imagined a proposal, in the last decade of the twentieth century, to admit that the homestead frontier was a bad mistake and to return the prairie to its natural grass as a thousand-square-mile refuge of antelope and rattlesnakes and hawks.

My mother is outraged. "What do you think of these guys who come in here from outside and want to turn all this ranchland into something they call the Big Open? I can tell you, the people who live out here don't think it's so empty. What do you think of moving out people who've lived on their land for five generations?"

I take my mother with me when I go to visit Mabel, who lives alone on Uncle Theo's old place down on Warm Spring Creek. For me it's like one of those dreams that recur often enough to seem familiar: the old wire gates in the corners of pastures, the narrow wheel ruts disappearing through grass into thin air. Where was the old graveled county road? I can't get my bearings.

My mother knows exactly where she is going. After all, she never left. She shows me where to turn off from the Denton highway, looks to see how the wheat is ripening on the bench, and leans forward expectantly as we crawl down that winding road into the cleft of the creek.

"Coming down here brings back good memories," she explains, and I know that she can see Aunt Em in her wrapper, opening the door of a house that no longer exists, welcoming the young people, and spreading bedding for them on the floor or on the couches when they ride in at three or four or five in the morning from one of the country dances. My mother met my father in Aunt Em's house.

Today Mabel comes out to meet us. She wears a cotton house-dress and anklets under her loafers, and her eyes are bright blue and her face is as deeply tanned as though she still got out and rode the combine during harvest. She could be fifty, not eighty.

Mabel and my father grew up together, practically. They were two of the "kidders" who came here to visit their uncle Theo and aunt Em, my father their nephew in fact and Mabel their surrogate daughter. After he married my mother, Mabel eventually married someone else, had three children, then raised them by herself and ran the ranch after her husband died. Now it's just Mabel at the table Aunt Em used to set for twenty for Sunday dinners.

Just inside her front gate grows the shaggy giant of a cotton-wood that Uncle Theo transplanted as a sprout in 1905, and Mabel tells me the story about how he saved it from being trampled by his brother's children by driving an ax handle into the ground beside it and tying it up. Mabel knows other stories I want to hear. Over iced tea and photograph albums, I try to get her to talk about a woman, a midwife, who once lived a few miles from here and ranched by herself. But Mabel doesn't remember much about the midwife, isn't interested in her.

But Irene Bartok—now, there's a real story, and one I ought to hear!

"You can still see the foundation rocks of Dancey's cabin, right up there on the hill," she says.

In the late afternoon, while my mother and Mabel stand by the gate and talk in the shadow of the hill, I wander across the road and try to remember the old log chicken-house, the sheep sheds, the old barn where Uncle Theo tried to hold down his cat population by keeping an old boot handy into which he stuffed tomcats, headfirst, to castrate them with his pocketknife. I have never liked being down here. I feel the suffocation of the early dusk closing down on the cleft, and I want to claw my way up to the rimrocks, where I can see what is coming.

What a short time this world of Uncle Theo's lasted, less than a hundred years, hardly more than fifty years. Most of the trees in his old orchard are dead. They were summer apples and crabapples, anyway, which no one cares enough for today to have for the picking, though they seemed so succulent to the homesteaders who drove down here with teams and wagons to buy fruit.

My mother and I have little to say in the car as I drive up the narrow road to the benchland, where the sun still shines. She has asked, "How is Imogene?" and I have tried to tell her, but sometimes I think my mother cannot imagine any of us out of the context of Fergus County. Imogene is still her big sis, Mary the seventeen-year-old who went away. Elizabeth, even Rachel—it is as though we are spinning in orbit around this center of hers, as incomprehensible to her as surplus moons.

Where the graveled road meets the paved highway, we turn west and drive the few miles past Aunt Carrie's old house to the Judith River bridge, where, in a cottonwood-shaded house trailer behind the original old house, my father's first cousin Myrtle still lives.

This is the old Sample place, and where the river widens below the bridge and flows shallow and easy is Sample's Crossing. From her tiny front lawn, Myrtle can see the current and the pale wads of cotton that float down from the giant trees that Uncle Theo planted as saplings in the mid-1880s. Other groves of Uncle Theo's trees can still be seen, along the highway between Denton and Lewistown, if you know where to look. They shade the ruins of the old Barney place, the old Pernot place. They are ancient for cottonwoods, they can't live much longer, but for now their shade is as pervasive as ever.

Myrtle welcomes us, brings us more iced tea, and shows us more photographs. Grandchildren, great-grandchildren. Old family poses. And a tinted enlargement, a copy of a picture that hangs in the Cowboy Hall of Fame, of her husband, Noisy, atop a bucking bronc at the old unfenced rodeo grounds at Alton.

I remember a photograph Mabel showed us earlier this afternoon, of herself and Myrtle as two-year-olds in immaculate white dresses, white bows in their hair, regarding each other with the implacable curiosity of toddlers, and I wonder if that curiosity has been sated by now, for Myrtle and Mabel have lived within five miles of each other for most of the twentieth century.

Myrtle's mother was Abe's daughter Carrie, the very first of the Montana-born children. Myrtle tells stories that Carrie told her, about life in the 1880s in that first log cabin that Abe built on the sage slope. Humdrum days with little change. Details. Carrie's mother, taking all the children berrying, stumbling upon a rattlesnake den. Carrie's mother, when a passing cowboy looked at the little girl's long black braids and remarked that it looked like she had some Indian in her—*Good thing Abe didn't hear him say that, or he would have killed him.*

Placid days in a dark frame. Sunlight enjoyed briefly and at great cost, always with a shadow hovering on the periphery. Myrtle catches my mother's eye. They both know a thing or two that I don't. They are two women who have measured their lives in blankets and sheets and blue jeans and shirts and dresses washed on a washboard, dried on a line, and sprinkled and ironed, and they will never again willingly wear any clothing that needs to be ironed.

The midwife? I ask.

Yes, Myrtle knew of her. Saw her once, right here at the crossing. She was bringing her cattle across the river, and she rode just like a man—"Swore just like a man, too," says Myrtle.

But Irene Bartok—now, there's the story! Like Mabel, Myrtle is eager to tell it, for it overlays her landscape like a myth of place, of the way she has lived in this place.

Oh, yes, Irene Bartok. Everybody thought she'd done it, but nobody could ever prove it. You see, they never found his body.

The prairie without a population is a desert, wrote another dreamer at about the same time Theo was adding the sheep shed and the long log chicken-house to his ranch buildings and stringing a barbed-wire telephone line between himself and his neighbors. James J. Hill would have agreed with Theo that all was possible, and, like Theo, Hill could visualize a transformed landscape. In 1909 he saw the Enlarged Homestead Act double the amount of free land a man or woman could stake out and prove up on, and he worked tirelessly to promote the settlement of the plains. Why not a family farm on every three hundred and twenty of Montana's dryland acres that would produce high-protein hard spring and winter wheat to be carried by Hill's railroads to markets all over the world?

In his mind's eye Theo saw the garden stronghold in his deep cleft. He saw the creek bed diverted and a slough formed where, in the winter, he would cut ice in eighteen-inch blocks, to store it through the summer in gunny sacks and sawdust in an ice house with heavy stone walls set well back into the side of the hill. Butter and cream would cool in his ice house, and hanging quarters of beef and mutton would supply his Sunday table.

While Theo and Em were building a generator that lit their house with flickering electricity for a few hours at night, Hill was writing, stumping, sending out advertising brochures and leaflets, giving prizes for sheaves of grain and fat cattle, financing research into deep plowing and intensive cultivation. He may have believed everything he wrote.

Do you dream of independence? Self-sufficiency? An empty prairie made productive by your labor? Fenced fields and neat farm buildings?

Do you really dream that you can impose yourself on this landscape?

In 1910 Uncle Theo and Aunt Em watched the population of Montana increase by nearly 40 percent. They sold apples and plums to the new neighbors, who had left lives in Chicago or New York or Norway or Czechoslovakia and come with their families and their bare necessities and keepsakes and pianos and rosemaling chests to hammer up tarpaper shacks on their three-hundred-and-twenties and scratch a first crop into the sod. Among the first of these new neighbors were the Welches, who had arrived on a train from Iowa in the spring of 1910 with their little girl, Sylva. Their second baby, Imogene, wasn't due until September.

The new town of Denton sprang up north of the Judith River to supply the newcomers with a post office and drug store, hotels and hardware and general merchandise and a livery stable. And the rains fell, and the wheat sprouted and ripened, beyond the wildest dreams of the new farmers—twenty, even twenty-five bushels to the acre—and yet they were unsurprised. Sudden good fortune was no more than they had been promised.

In 1917 less rain fell. *Hang on another year.* If we get into the Great War, it ought to raise the price of wheat, at least. We're bound to get rain in the fall. Bound to get rain next spring. And, renewing the notes they had signed at the bank for their shacks and plows, borrowing money to live on, the homesteaders hung on through 1918 and 1919. But the price of wheat fell after the war, and the drought spread until, in 1920, dust clouds rolled over the hundreds of thousands of acres of new cultivation, and the little children who had been born in Montana saw fields where nothing grew.

It was a matter of brief interest for Uncle Theo and Aunt Em as well as for their neighbors to hear that Joe Dancey was getting married. How old was he? He had been an old bachelor for so long, holed up in that dank cabin of his, where the sod grew as thick on his pole roof as it did on the ground, why would he want to bother with a wife now? As for the Bartok girl, her folks were starving out. Maybe they wanted one less mouth to feed.

The Bartoks had come from the old country in 1914 and filed a claim on a strip of high ground. The old man was ornery, as the women put it. Irene grew up to be a big girl with a red face and black raisins of eyes, and she wore her black curly hair in braids until she left home and went to live in Denton, in a room over the livery stable. Then she bobbed her hair. Released of its weight, it rose in the wind when she walked in the early evenings, down the plank walks of Denton or out to the homestead to see her mother. How was she supporting herself? Though it seemed never to be spoken of, Uncle Theo and Aunt Em both knew what she was thought to be.

What could be said for Irene? She had gone to school until she was sixteen, the legal age; she got what Fergus County had to offer. True, she had never been one of the boys and girls who gathered at Theo's house for meetings of the 4-H Club, where Em taught the girls to cook and sew and Theo taught them to judge cattle and raise poultry and practice horticulture right along with the boys. Childless, Theo and Em loved their neighbors' children and their many nieces and nephews.

But not Irene Bartok, she had never hung around, never learned to tease her uncle Theo or hear his explosive "Dot durn it, kidder!" The Bartoks were still too close to the old country, that was part of the reason. Catholic, of course.

And old man Bartok liked to keep his girls at home and working hard. Irene may have had her reasons for moving to Denton.

The schoolteacher, Mrs. Welch, had finished correcting papers and was about ready to blow out her lamp and go to bed when somebody pounded on her door.

She glanced up. It was after ten o'clock, but she had been living by herself in teacherages too long to feel anxious after dark. She capped her pen and opened the door on the January night.

The two chattering women nearly knocked her down in their panicky haste to get through her door and inside the lighted teacherage. Mrs. Welch knew them: Irene Bartok and her mother.

"What in the world is the matter?" she asked them.

At first they could not speak; they were wringing their hands and crying like small children, frightened out of their wits, though they looked as stout as two trolls in their headscarves and their woolen coats buttoned over their protruding stomachs.

"For goodness sake, sit down and stop your bawling," said Mrs. Welch in the voice she used for children, "or they'll hear you all the way to Denton."

For some reason that idea brought fresh tears and recriminations, not all in English, between the mother and daughter. Mrs. Welch sighed and went to poke up her fire to bring her kettle to a boil.

Sipping strong hot tea, shaking, they finally were able to tell their tale. They had been walking home from Denton, Irene said, when they noticed a light following them, low, on the horizon—

"Headlights," said Mrs. Welch.

No! Not headlights. A single bluish light, wavering over the tips of sagebrush that pocked the fresh snow, following them, slowing when they stopped, catching up easily when they broke into a run—

"Drink your tea," urged Mrs. Welch, struck in spite of herself at the thought of these two running all the way from Denton from a blue light. Irene was bigger than her mother, but they both were as broad and solid as brood sows, with their bulbous faces and breasts. Remembering the rumors, Mrs. Welch looked more carefully at Irene, but the girl was too fat and too closely buttoned into her coat for Mrs. Welch to know whether she was pregnant.

Maybe they'd imagined the light?

No! They both shook their heads, certain of what they had seen. Mrs. Welch thought that Irene's eyes were as opaque as buttons and yet bottomless, like a hunted thing's, and in spite of all the talk she had heard, all the speculation about what had really happened to Joe Dancey, she felt a stir of pity.

When they had drained their third cups of tea, Mrs. Welch saw them to the door. It was nearly midnight by now, and the cold of late January had settled in hoarfrost on the planks, which shone as far as the light reached. Mrs. Welch could see the dim line of fence posts leaning over the snow, and the outline of the road which faded in one direction toward Denton and in the other direction toward the remote Bartok shack, and nothing else for miles except the prairie, faintly white to the horizon, and the endless revolving constellations.

No moon, she remembered. It could not have been the moon that had followed the two women and whatever guilty secret they were carrying. But she only said, "You see? There's nothing out there. You'll be all right now."

Mrs. Welch stood on her doorstep with her warm lamplight falling through the open door for a few feet across the snow and watched the two dark shapes retreating until they were hardly more significant than the shapes of the fence posts they followed. Although she would have been very surprised to see a mysterious blue light following low along the snowline, she waited, crossing her arms against the pervasive cold, until she could no longer distinguish the two small dark blobs even by their movement, before she turned thankfully back into the teacherage and closed the door.

The midwife was a youngish woman who had trained as a nurse at St. Joseph's Hospital in Lewistown but had gotten fed up with clinical routine and the discipline of the nuns. Now she lived by herself on her place on dry Plum Creek, miles down the Judith River from anybody else, but she would throw a saddle on a horse, lash her black bag behind her by the saddle strings, and ride to the bedside of anybody who needed her. Whether they could pay or not, no matter who they were, if they really needed her.

So she didn't hesitate when one of Irene's little sisters walked down the trail through the river breaks to tell her that Irene's water had broken. She turned the calf in with the milk cow to keep until she got back, threw a short loop over the head of her lanky brown gelding and told him to quit his goddamn snorting, cinched her saddle down tight, tied on her doctor's bag, and swung up.

The gelding pranced, threatening to bog his head and buck, but she just warned him she'd goddamn break him in half if he didn't settle down, and laid her quirt on him. The late-May sun was warm enough that, by the time she had ridden up the trail as high as the jack pines that split the sandstone rim, the gelding was sweating and glad enough to level out in his ground-eating trot.

Hell, thought the midwife, she hadn't been up here in a coon's age. Four or five years ago Joe Dancey had split his foot open with an ax, and she had ridden up and stitched him back together. She had thought then that Joe showed the breed in him as he got older, the furrows in his face deepening and his nose getting sharper. But she hadn't minded Joe Dancey if he was a breed, he had been decent enough in his own way.

The cabin, when it came in view above the rimrocks, didn't look any different from the way it had five years ago, with gray logs sagging off the plumb and bunchgrass growing on the roof. The empty corral. No signs of life, not even a clothesline. Not even an outhouse. Likely they had kept a pot under the bed at night and went out in the sagebrush with a shovel in the daytime. Certainly the sagebrush rolled on and on. A mile away, the midwife could see the tips of the pines growing in the ravine that led down to Theo Hogeland's place and, miles beyond the ravine, the pale blue of the South Moccasins. She wondered how Irene had gotten in and out for mail and groceries—walked, she guessed.

The midwife swung down from the saddle and tied her gelding to a corral post where he could nip at last year's dry grass growing untrampled around the posts and in the wagon ruts and adding to the general air of abandonment. She loosened the cinch, thinking she could always come out later and unsaddle him and turn him into the corral if it looked as if she was going to be here all night. Then she hoisted her black bag and strode the few yards to the cabin.

At first she thought the door was locked. She rattled the doorknob—it was a real knob, with a faceplate Dancey had chiseled a notch for and screwed into the solid plank of the door frame—before she realized that, no, something heavy had been shoved up against the door from the inside.

"Irene!" she yelled. "Are you in there?"

No answer.

The midwife listened. All she could hear was the wind that never stopped ragging at the sagebrush and, back at the corral,

the jingle of her horse's bridle chains as he stretched for grass.
And yet somehow she was certain that somebody was in the cabin.

"Irene!" she bellowed. "Open up!" And she gave the door a
good square kick with her bootheel, and it budged maybe a quarter
of an inch.

"Irene, you stupid bitch, let me in!"

She hauled off with another battery of kicks on the door, *bam
bam bam bam bam,* and forced it open another inch. Now she could
see the barrel and the chest of drawers that had been shoved up
as a barricade, the musty darkness on both sides of the narrow
crack of light, and, cowering back in the bed in the farthest corner,
a terrified white face.

"Who's gonna take care of her and the kid? You?" the midwife
asked the little sister, who had finally arrived on foot and helped
her coax Irene to shift the furniture from in front of the door.

"I guess."

The midwife shook her head. Irene would be all right, nothing
could kill her, but the baby was undersized and blue. She had
bathed and diapered and swaddled him in clothes sent over by
Irene's mother, and she had shown Irene how to feed him.

"Listen, I got cow's milk," the midwife told the little sister.
"All you gotta do is ask."

It was the fetid air in the windowless cabin that was getting to
her, that and the lack of anything to make do with. The midwife
had seen plenty of misery. She had seen children she suspected
were going hungry. She knew their parents were. Her own cow's
milk tasted of weeds.

Still—"Goddamn it to hell, Irene, you gotta pull yourself together!'' she shouted. "Do you understand what I'm telling you?''

But she knew she might as well be yelling at the bedposts. Irene stared back at her, slack-faced and sweating. The only thing on Irene's mind was her fear.

It was the little sister who told, after the baby died, that it had been born with the print of a boot in its face, where Dancey had kicked Irene.

Likelier to have been old man Bartok who had kicked her, thought Mrs. Welch. After he found out she was pregnant, he wouldn't let her stay at home any longer. Where could she go but back to the cabin on the high prairie she thought was haunted?

And so the story becomes a kind of communal novel, with twenty or more voices contributing their fragments of the known events, another hundred voices in the chorus, and one of the voices mine, retelling and revising, until the shifting truth spreads its own wings and casts the long shadow of fiction. Irene and her mother killed him, of course. They probably buried him out on the prairie on the November night Lud Lind met them.

Truth: Mrs. Welch—*When they knocked at the teacherage door that night, they were so terrified of the light they thought was following them that Ma thought she'd never get them calmed down*—never advanced a theory as to what the blue light might have been. Mrs. Welch had been teaching for nearly fifteen years to support her family. She seldom lived with her husband, whom she blamed for the failure of their homestead. After his death she lived alone for another thirty years. She had earned enough by her own hard work to help her daughters and her granddaughters through college. Learn to stand on your own two feet, she warned us all.

Truth: The midwife—*Furniture was pushed up against the door, so she couldn't even get in to deliver the baby until she coaxed Irene to shift it*—was a woman named Edna Maguire who lived by herself on Plum Creek for years. She ran cattle and sheep, but she would saddle a horse and ride with her black bag if anybody needed her.

One time a man on the lower Judith raped a woman, and afterward somebody caught him and castrated him. He didn't know who covered his head with a sack and held him down, but later it was seen that he was cut and bandaged professionally, so Edna Maguire got the credit for it. But nobody ever knew for sure.

She suffered from dementia in her last years. While she waited to die in St. Joseph's Hospital in Lewistown, where long ago she had trained as a nurse, a man named Pete Daniels, whom she had been living with down on Plum Creek—*Pete Daniels was an Indian, but he was a good old Indian*—used to bring her bunches of the tough yellow blooms from the dry hillsides. Balsamroot, her favorite flower.

When the young people rode in at three or four or five in the morning after the schoolhouse dances, Aunt Em was always there in her wrapper to spread beds for the girls and the married couples on the couches or on the floor and to direct the single men out to the bunkhouse. When the kids woke up at noon on Sunday, she would cook breakfast for everybody. A crowd of young people around was just what Em liked.

It was at these lazy Sunday breakfasts in the early winter that Em heard the first unalarming talk. Somebody guessed that Joe Dancey had disappeared again. Well, that wasn't unusual, Joe was always dropping out of sight, and usually at the start of cold weather. And yet there was bound to be a last time. Would it be so strange if Joe never came back from one of his disappearances?

The part that struck the manager of the feed store in Denton as pretty damn funny was that Dancey had worked for him for a couple weeks, unloading grain, but he had never come back to collect his wages. The money still lay right there in the desk drawer.

Sitting around Aunt Em's breakfast table, the young men got to talking. Hadn't Dancey and Irene been at that dance at Alton, clear last November?

"—they sure as hell weren't there when we got ready to leave, because Dancey'd tied his team in the barn alongside mine, and they were gone when I went out to hitch up—"

A more ominous story made the neighborhood rounds.

"—remember? She was with him at the dance. But later, maybe three in the morning, Lud Lind was taking a shortcut home when he met Irene and her mother—"

"Were they alone?"

"Alone where they had no business being at three in the morning."

Pondering, Em herself may have felt unsubstantial. Looking out the kitchen window at Theo's snowbound garden, at the faint humps where, in a few months, the green spikes would be breaking out in rows of Theo's favorite gladioli opening into stiff pink and red and yellow stalks, hundreds, from which he would choose the largest and most perfect to cut for his horticulture booth at the Fergus County Fair, on whose board he served—for just the moment it took to draw another breath, Em may have felt as though the gladioli, the garden, the Fergus County Fair, and she and Theo and everything they had wrought together were transparent; as though, if she looked quickly enough, she could see through all their labors to what had gone before or was to come.

After the episode of the blue light, the speculation about Irene got to the point where Uncle Theo cranked up his telephone and called together a few of his neighbors over the barbed-wire line. Bundled warmly, the men met at his place and piled into a Model T, which easily negotiated the steep pitch of the road up through the rimrocks. They said little, their breaths hung in white clouds around their muffled faces. The country fell behind them, shrouded pines and endless snowy stretches of bluffs and buttes and benchland, enormous enough to swallow up the crawling black Model T and everyone in it.

The communal novel follows in the narrow tracks of the Model T, documents its arrival at the cabin. Like a wide-angle lens without a soundtrack, it shows the men getting out and looking around at the fresh snow, the empty corral, the curl of smoke from the stovepipe. It follows the men, broad and bulky and responsible in their overcoats as they approach the cabin door, but it will not follow them inside that door.

"—Uncle Theo and some other men went up and looked around, but they couldn't find anything to make them think they should call the sheriff—"

Where was Joe's horse? His saddle? What about the team and wagon he had driven to the dance? And what did Irene have to say about the dance, and its aftermath, or about her long walk with her mother on the prairie in the waning night?

The communal novel doesn't want to know. The price Irene paid is its story, and there it stops.

Idaho, November 1991

East of town, sunk deep enough among the fields that you don't see it until you come upon it, is a reservoir called Mann's Lake, which is also a bird refuge. When I park my car at the barbed-wire fence and get out, hundreds of Canada geese rise from the surface of the water and yelp off into the colorless sky.

Already it is nearly four in the afternoon, and I know I don't have much daylight left. The water is low for November, and already it is losing its red sheen as the sun drops lower through the overcast, though a groundrow of willows to the east has briefly turned ruddy. The air is colder than I thought, but I walk down the muddy incline to the water. With the high mud banks all around me, it's like being at the bottom of a bowl. Tracks of geese and herons, dog tracks—and beer cans everywhere, and signs of bonfires.

I follow the waterline until I come up against riprap too steep and too unstable to walk across. The ducks seem unalarmed, trailing their long wakes across the surface until I get too close, and then they scud for deeper water. The geese circle again, wanting to land. Such a wild sound, such an anachronism.

Just before we committed her to sedation and the locked north wing, Brian did a kind thing for Imogene. He brought her out here to Mann's Lake for the afternoon and walked with her along the water and helped her to spot birds through a pair of binoculars. Today I look at the water and the mud and the geese through her eyes, knowing as she did not know what she was seeing for the last time.

Story and how to tell it is on my mind—Imogene's story, and Lud Lind's, and mine—and another fall afternoon, another time and place. The cottonwoods along the Milk River in northern Montana had lost their leaves, as I remember, and the aspens had turned drab—but my memory is a deceiving spirit, and I was sitting in the cab of a pickup truck with a man I was not married to for what I knew was the last time.

I will borrow a name for him. Pete Daniels.

8

/ / /

Back in January and February of 1991, after we had moved Imogene over to the Villa Villekula, and during those weeks that she sat rocking back and forth in her wheelchair with her eyes fixed inward, waiting while the sedatives slowly drained out of her system, Elizabeth and I stared each other in the face like the survivors of a wreck. What were we to do next?

Elizabeth had lost more weight, and her eyes were as white-ringed, her neck as arched and tense as a nervous mare's. She wasn't feeling well, nothing seemed to stay in her stomach, and she shied away from the reports I brought back from my visits to Imogene. Both of us were haunted by the specter of an Imogene who, somehow ascending back through the black hole of her mind, would demand an accounting from us: *Where is everything? My dog, my life? Why have you done this to me?*

What to do with my aunt's possessions that we had packed in Port Angeles only last June and carted back to Idaho with us? My attorney had advised me not to sell her house as long as there was the faintest chance of her returning to live there, and though I knew at heart that there was not the faintest chance, it was advice I wanted to follow. So Elizabeth and Brian would go on living there for the time being. Eventually, maybe, we would clear it out and rent it out. And so, for the second time in seven months, Elizabeth and I sorted through Auntie's clothes and books and junk while Rachel carried armloads to the trash or out to the trunk of the car to haul down to the Salvation Army.

Finally, postponing decisions, trying to pretend we were actually accomplishing something, we rummaged through her desk drawers.

"Did you know that she kept a diary?" Elizabeth asked me one morning.

"No," I said.

"Well, she did. I found her diaries last night."

At first I didn't believe her. Elizabeth went and got a cardboard box from my aunt's bedroom and set it down on the kitchen table, and I lifted out the little volumes. Leatherbound five-year diaries, the kind with clasps and locks. They started with the shiny gold-stamped ones on top and went down to the small scuffed ones at the bottom of the box. Eleven of them.

"I read a little, here and there," said Elizabeth.

I was still feeling disbelief. "How far back do they go?"

"Nearly fifty years. To 1933. I don't think she ever missed a day."

"From 1933 until—"

"Until the day we moved her here. That's where she stopped."

I picked up one of the little books at random and opened it. The closely written lines in my aunt's familiar handwriting leaped out at me, and I shut it again. *Diaries?* In all the times I stayed with her, did I ever remember her writing in a diary?

A flicker of a memory, once, when we were traveling together—a brief jotting—*Don't turn the light off yet, I want to finish this—*

Of course, that would have been her pattern. The few lines, last thing at night, written in bed. But how could I not have known about that pattern in a woman I thought I knew so well?

"I felt so sad, reading," Elizabeth was saying. "She was so unhappy. I never knew she was unhappy."

The words chased themselves around my brain. What could Elizabeth mean? Auntie unhappy? Until the cruel blows of the past seven months, she had always seemed to me the merriest, the stablest woman I knew. All those late nights in Port Angeles while a log fire shot reflections against the window that looked out on the dark strait, while I told her the surface of my grief and took comfort from the rising haze of her cigarette. Her dark ironic eyes as she listened to what I chose to tell. Always sympathizing, always on my side—what had she really been thinking? No! Of course she had been happy; otherwise, what about my secret belief that, if only I tried harder to be like her, to pare my life down as she had to its essentials of teaching and gardening and love of children, I would be spared pain?

Elizabeth, unaware of my disquiet, was talking about something—about birthdays. "Auntie always seemed so pleased with each new baby in the family. Always seemed to love us so much. So I started looking up all our birthdays to see what she said when we were born. And I was so surprised! She never says a word!''

"Oh really!" I said.

Pulling myself back into the present, I found Auntie's diary for 1939, turned to December 10, then leafed over a few pages to December 14, and read the entry aloud to Elizabeth. *Got a card from Doris that Mary Rebecca arrived last Sunday—weight 8 lb 15 oz. I am so excited I can hardly wait.*

"She had to wait a few days until the card came in the mail," I explained.

Elizabeth looked blank. "Card?" Then she caught herself, realized what she was assuming. Well, of course, they wouldn't phone! The old barbed-wire neighborhood lines were pretty much inoperable by 1939, and Bell Telephone did not run its lines out into Fergus County until after World War II, and even then nobody was in the habit of spending money on long-distance telephoning when they could stick a three-cent stamp on a letter.

I looked up Elizabeth's birthday—September 28, 1961—and then showed her the entry for October 4. *Baby card from Mary— Elizabeth Mary. Born the 28th. I'm so glad. . . . Oh I wish I could see her!*

Elizabeth took the diary from me and reread the entry about her birth, while I thought about the distance between my generation and hers, whose vital news arrives on a long-distance line and fades so quickly.

"What do you want to do with her diaries?" she asked after a while.

"I suppose I'll read them," I said.

/ / /

How can I read her diaries when she is still alive, after a fashion? But, like a voyeur, drawn by something stronger than curiosity, I riffle pages, reading entries that evoke what I already know.

Late June of 1947, for example. *Sun. Took Mary swimming. . . . Current swift but Mary is not at all scared. . . . Jack showed us a good swimming hole. It is fine—good bottom—deep—not too fast a current. . . . Mary floated at last.*

I was seven years old in June 1947, and I was a little dryland girl. I had never been swimming, never seen more water than the Judith River, which I'd been told to stay away from, never even taken a bath in anything bigger than a galvanized washtub, and now here I stood in ankle-deep current while Spring Creek sparkled over the gravel in the sun and reflected its light into my eyes. I knew that my father's uncles used to swim in this hole, and that they had tried to teach my father to swim, but he had refused. Solid ground was for him. Now Auntie stood up to her waist in her black bathing suit and white rubber cap in the deep hole under the willows, calling to me. The dark-green water concealed the lower half of her, cutting her off at the waist and reflecting back her top half, white cap and black suit, as though she had been split and then fused as a woman with two heads and four arms.

Even with two heads, she didn't know that I was terrified? Probably not. I had been taught as surely as she had not to let on. Wade in and try to float, even if you're scared to death.

What about her own fears?

Here is her entry for June 16, 1942. *This is a day I'll never forget. Jack's birthday. We planned cherry pie & rice pudding for supper. I got thrown into the wheel of the mower & badly cut. We handled the situation calmly.*

Imogene's mowing-machine accident. My father used to tell me his version of that morning. It had shaken him profoundly. He and my mother were young, still in their twenties, and I think now that Imogene's accident may have been their first real awakening to inevitability.

Imogene had gone out to mow hay with my father's team of flashy sorrel colts. Socks and Babe, a bald-faced gelding and a blaze-faced mare, still flashy and still spooky-eyed in their old age, when I remember them. Their names evoke a lost life along the Judith River, where the war on the other side of the world was forcing up prices and making scarcities, but where the Montana-born boys and girls like my father and mother were scratching a living out of the gumbo that had worn out their parents.

Imogene had closed her school that spring and come to help get the hay in. She had braided her hair that morning, and worn Levi's and a white shirt—I know, because one of my earliest memories is of her propped in the back seat of her own car with her foot packed in towels after the sorrel colts had run away with her and pitched her off the high seat of the mowing machine and down, somehow, into the sickle bar. Those shining iron teeth had bitten into her ankle, nearly all the way around, in a deep gouge to the bone that would leave her crippled for months and scarred for the rest of her life.

We handled it calmly. My father, raking hay in another field, glanced across the coulee and saw that Imogene hadn't finished her round. He unhitched his own team, jumped on one of his horses bareback, and tore the quarter of a mile across cutbanks and hayfields to find Imogene sitting in blood-soaked grass with her own shoelace tied around her ankle for a tourniquet—"and a damn good thing she knew what to do, because I sure the hell wouldn't have got there in time." She had even managed to catch the sorrel colts and tie them to a fence post.

My father galloped back to the house and got Imogene's car. He and my mother packed her foot and lifted her into the back seat to drive her the thirty miles over a gravel road to Lewistown—not before I had climbed into the front seat to look over it, confused by the adult voices and the smell of blood. Auntie laughed when she saw my face. "Look what they've done to me, Mary!" Then somebody, perhaps my mother, lifted me down from the car and set me howling inside the wire fence.

My father and mother drove Imogene to Lewistown. It would have taken an hour on bald wartime tires, with dust rising and settling and the song of meadowlarks floating back into oblivion from fence posts along the highway. Imogene and my parents would hardly have spoken. They all knew what the worst was likely to be. But at the cool sandstone archway of little St. Joseph's Hospital the nuns ran out to meet them and carry Imogene inside. Sister St. Paul and Dr. Solterro went to work with sutures and, against all their own expectations, in a desperate operation that returned to Imogene nearly fifty years later when, hospitalized for an arteriogram, she wandered into a time warp where those sensations and fragments of detail still lived as fresh as in 1942, they succeeded in saving her foot.

From the perspective of years, I always thought the crucial point about the mowing-machine accident—*This is a day I'll never forget* —was that it forced Imogene to leave a dead-end life of teaching for seventy or eighty dollars a month in the rural schools of central Montana. It was an uncertain living—the school boards, unwilling to grant tenure, rarely kept a teacher more than a year or two— and an isolated and strenuous one. The country schoolteachers could hope one of the neighbors remembered to bring them their mail or give them a ride to town for groceries, and meanwhile they were expected to carry their own coal and water, sweep out their schools and dust and clean their blackboards, and get out in the schoolyard at recess and play baseball or pom-pom-pullaway with the kids. Who'd hire a teacher without one foot?

"I couldn't get a job close to home that fall. Everybody in Fergus County had heard how badly I was hurt, and none of the school boards would even *look* at me," my aunt always told me, "so I applied at schools where nobody had heard of me." Out in Washington, where the war industry was rolling at full speed and teachers were leaving their classrooms to take the new high-paying jobs in the shipyards, she found a school superintendent willing to take a chance on a woman from Montana on crutches.

But in the immediacy of that moment, she saw what mattered at a closer focus. *This is a day I'll never forget.* The reason everybody always remembered the date of Imogene's accident was that it was my father's birthday. Cherry pie was his favorite, and they had been planning to have cherry pie for supper that night.

The precious trivial. My aunt's diaries are filled like a ragbag with the daily doings that make up a life. She hardly ever writes more than a line or two, but she notes which night she made muffins for supper—*they were good*—what the children fought about in school—*kids were mean as dirt today*—or which exact evening in 1939 she finished crocheting the wool afghan that even now lies in tatters in my back closet while I try to make up my mind to throw it out.

To read the diaries is to experience the absolutely linear. A plot of sorts emerges, like a river, continuous, with apparently unrelated details bobbing to the surface and then submerging. Names of characters appear in these pages without reason or description, then disappear in the same way. I learn to read between the lines, filling in with what I already know. Faces loom up, voices speak from the margins. What is most compelling is the immediacy. She is writing *right now*. She is twenty-three, and my mother is nineteen, and they can't see ahead the way I can when I glance down the page.

What she could see was the past. How could she bear it? She used the five-year format, so that a given page contains five entries for five consecutive years; she could take in at a glance what she had hoped for the year before, or the year before that, or what she had dreaded.

She is place-specific. I could draw a map of that thirty-mile radius, re-create its textures out of memory. *I want that pink suit I saw in Power's, size eighteen, but I can't afford it*—and instantly I see the main street of Lewistown, Montana, the way it descends down the cottonwood-shaded hill, past the old junior-high school and the courthouse to the two or three commercial blocks, the six-story white marble Montana Building, and the overpainted sandstone building occupied at present by a chain clothing store whose racks of marked-down western wear and special-order blue jeans exist simultaneously in my mind with the dignified clerks, the gracious aisles, and the molded tin ceilings of the old T. C. Power's Mercantile Company.

Or: *Going home, we got stuck on the bottom last night*—and I could walk to that precise mudhole, even at night in a rainstorm; I know just where the dirt road leaves the highway and curves across a treacherous stretch of gumbo toward the cottonwood-log house where my father and mother lived during the early 1940s, and where the neighbors, the long-dead, reappear in a context where getting stuck, getting high-centered, getting a flat tire, is a commonplace of every drive in a car—*Saw Art and Esther, they were stuck; Saw Sid and Carrie Killham*—just as I could walk to the precise swimming hole my father showed Imogene—*Good bottom—deep— not too fast a current*—if it still lay in that willow-shaded bend in Spring Creek.

But it doesn't. The land has been sold and sold again, and the creek has been bulldozed and straightened, and the willows have been gouged out, and the current has flooded its new banks and turned meadows to bogs when the dream that we tried to impose on landscape went ugly. Nothing is still there, not the swimming hole, not the cattle crossing, not the woman in the white bathing cap who calls to the child in the shallows.

Other entries trouble me. I will never know their context. On August 11, 1949, my aunt apparently was planning a vacation trip back to Montana. *Letter from Ma. She wants to meet me in a hotel for a day. Damn it, I hate my family to just tear me in pieces.*

So I had thought I knew something about Imogene's life, and about that certain place in Montana, closed among the low mountains and straitened by the economic circumstances of the 1930s and the early 1940s, where she came to young womanhood. Now I wonder what I do know, and how much of that is my own fiction, and how much was hers, after the revelations of those inexorable lines, scrawled day after day for almost fifty years in Imogene's diaries.

I now believe that it was not the near loss of her foot to the sickles that altered her, but an earlier episode in Imogene's life that drew her deep into an emotional attachment to my father and my mother and me. Her diary entries for the last two or three years she lived in Montana increasingly note the details of her younger sister's life and her dependence upon her sister's family. *Stopped to see Doris & Mary & promised to come down for dinner on Sunday. . . . Doris & I wrangled horses & watched the men break horses. . . . Got the pictures of Mary. Must start an album soon. . . . The men did not find the horses & we are worried about them. . . . It rained all night & day. Jack had to drive my car up to the road for me. I rode Pardner for him to ride back.*

And with what abandon she loved me, her sister's baby: *Doris gets breakfast & I bathe Mary. When she got tired she brot me her bottle & held up her arms to be taken. . . . Mary sure likes her Aunty Gene. . . . Mary was sure glad to see me. She gives little snorts of pleasure & satisfaction.*

I now think I know something about Imogene's isolation, and why she turned to my mother and father and me for emotional support. I think that perhaps the most profound effect of the mowing-machine accident—a truly accidental effect—was that it severed her bond with my mother and father as surely as it nearly severed her foot. I think that the accident freed her for another kind of isolation, this time self-imposed.

But I am interrupted in my deep reading by Elizabeth, who has made an appointment with an internist. She thinks she may have an ulcer.

Between the strain over Auntie and the uncertainty of her application to veterinary school, Elizabeth has quivered between tears and anger all winter. I walk with care around her, thinking before I speak, unwilling to risk an explosion. Could I have been so driven at her age? So racked with frustration?

My friends exclaim at how much Elizabeth looks like me. "Unbelievable! Like twins!" She and I both try to see the resemblance and fail. I recognize only her eyes; we both inherited my father's blue eyes. But though Elizabeth is an inch taller than I, she is much more finely drawn, and her wrists and ankles are narrower than Rachel's at age eight. And her coloring is subtler than mine. I could never pick out clothes for her, even when she was small, until I realized that she preferred the hazier shades, would never wear my bright reds and blues.

Elizabeth. Thorn in my side. When I was about the age she is now, I was divorcing her father, and she was ten, and tears rolled down her face when I told her, though she never cried aloud. And so she was part of the price I paid for myself.

But now she telephones me, sobbing so hard that at first I cannot understand her. "I'm not ready for this!" she keeps choking out, until at last she manages to tell me that the internist she consulted about an ulcer gave her a routine pregnancy test that has turned out to be positive.

What am I to say?

What was I to say to the ten-year-old? Did I understand enough in those days about the force of my own submerged currents to explain to anyone, let alone to my daughter, that I would have exploded if I had stayed with her father? How could I possibly have told her about the recurring dream in which he took me in his arms, smiling fondly, and squeezed and squeezed until, still smiling fondly, he had cracked my ribs and choked the breath out of me?

Thinking of these things, and about the resentments that have kept Elizabeth and me apart for so many years, I take a deep breath and speak the truth.

"If it were me, I'd certainly rather have a baby than an ulcer."

"But what about vet school?" she sobs. "How am I going to *do* this? This is my best chance, I've got to be accepted this time, and if I am, I'll be starting in late August. That's just when this baby is due. Mother, I'm not ready for a baby!"

What does she want to hear me say? All I can think about is late-September rain and the slick stone steps behind the old St. Joseph's Hospital in Lewistown, Montana, at two in the morning. I am twenty-one again. I hold a suitcase in one hand and a textbook in the other. My mother has just dropped me off at the curb and turned around to drive back to the ranch to stay with my two-year-old son. I start to climb the flight of steps toward the light over the door.

Who is ever ready?

"Your first baby?" says the night nurse who signs me in.

"No, my second."

Her manner changes instantly. "How far apart are your pains? Oh, God! Where's Sister?"

A few minutes later I hear her calling down the corridor: "Where's Sister? This baby is *coming,* and I can't find Sister!"

All I care is that apparently I am not going to have to face another twenty-four-hour labor on my own. What I mainly know about birthing is that it is lonely. Last time they told my young husband that he might as well go back to the ranch and get some sleep, and then they gave me an enema and a shave and left me alone all night in one of those echoing high-ceilinged rooms, where the only distraction was the occasional rumble of gurney wheels outside the door with another woman groaning, or a nurse glancing

in to check my dilation and leaving again. This time my husband
has gone back to Missoula to start the fall term without me. But
this time I've come prepared; I've brought my book.

I really do need to be reading, because I'm missing my first
week of classes at the University of Montana to have this baby.
It's my last year of undergraduate school, and I hate getting off to
a bad start, but I've sent my husband around to all my professors
to explain my absence and pick up my assignments. The professors
do a certain amount of tsk-tsking, because this is 1961, and they
don't yet know a thing about the women who, in another twenty
years, will flock back to college with their children slung on their
backs or dropped off at the day care, or who, like one of my
sisters, will go into labor during registration at Montana State
University, run over to the hospital, have her baby, and then run
back to the field house to pay her fees.

But in 1961 I'm an aberration, which is no bad thing. I'm not
a trend, I'm not a threat, in fact I'm so improbable that I am
easily overlooked. I can dive in and out of classes and swap babies
with my husband in time for him to get to his night job at the
lumber mill, and nobody notices.

"Oh, your poor husband! How does he stand it?" groans my
adviser when I bring him my class schedule with my twenty-two
credits to have him sign, but we both know his groan is only a
matter of form. After all, it is 1961, and I won't come across a
copy of *The Feminine Mystique* for another five or six years. I agree
with my adviser that it is my husband's education that matters,
that it is I who should be working nights to support us both, that
this sideshow act of mine with babies and twenty-two credits is,

at best, beside the point and, at worst, a hazard to everybody's peace of mind. I agree, I agree! It's just that I can't seem to stop.

But why, I might well ask myself as, my belly a contorted knot, I lean against the admissions desk and gasp and listen to the frantic nurse running up and down the corridor—"Where's Sister? Where's Sister?"—why am I having this baby? The first baby, okay, a bad mistake, my husband and I were teenagers in a stranglehold of lust and impatience and ignorance. But a second baby? Come on! I'm twenty-one years old now, soberer than I will be at fifty, and, besides, I've got a diaphragm.

Why? The only reason I can come up with is that I want her. As I will want still another baby, only it will take me twenty-one years and another man before I can have Rachel.

What to say to Elizabeth, who simultaneously sobs over the telephone and rushes to be born so fast that I'm not going to have to endure the indignity of an enema, won't have to grow back the itching, prickling stubble of my pubic hair after the shave? *Does she want to get rid of it?* Is that the sensible decision? Is that what she wants to hear from me?

My heart is in my mouth. The truth is all I can think to speak. "A new baby. I feel so happy."

I'm so glad. . . . I can hardly wait to see her.

And so Elizabeth rushed into the world after an hour's labor, and she has never slowed down from that rush, though her tiny footprints inked on the hospital's fancy certificate are narrow as a bird's, half the size of Rachel's birthprints. She slept in a hamper with handles that her father often carried with him or left on the back seat of the car while he fished the trout streams around

Missoula and occasionally ran back to the car to check on her. Soon she was standing behind him as he fished. She grew up to adore him.

When she was fourteen, I met the man who would become Rachel's father. "If you don't quit going out with him, I'll leave home! I'll go live with my father!" she hurtled at me.

I didn't. She did.

How long has Elizabeth wanted to be a veterinarian? Ever since I can remember. "An animal doctor," as she said in second grade.

Animals around the house, always. The little old beagle we got while her father and I were in graduate school in Missouri. The Siamese tomcat named Grinch that the man I call Pete Daniels gave me after we moved back to Montana, to Havre. A mama cat named Victoria, because she was so fecund.

Screams in the night—I turn on my bedside light in a panic. Elizabeth stands in my bedroom door with blood in her hair.

"The cat's having kittens in my bed!"

I follow her across the hall and into her bedroom, and, sure enough, there's Victoria sprawled across Elizabeth's pillow in a mess of blood and mucus and wet kittens. The last kitten spurts out from under her tail just as we get there.

"Here's the one I threw." Elizabeth brings a tiny blind kitten from across the room. "She was having them in my hair. I felt something wet on my ear, and I put up my hand, and it was *alive*. And I just threw it."

We return the kitten, mewling but otherwise undamaged, to Victoria. She licks it off, along with the other four, then coils around her litter while they nurse. She purrs up at us, as proud as if she were the first cat in the world ever to think of having a litter of kittens.

We decide to let the cats have Elizabeth's bed for the night. I take Elizabeth into the bathroom and wash her hair and let her curl up, toweled and damp as one of the new kittens, in my bed with me.

As a child Elizabeth is fearless. (How can I be so sure? I remember that diary entry—*Mary is not at all scared.*) Well, certainly Elizabeth seems fearless. She climbs a fence, and from the fence to the bare back of a neighbor's grazing horse, from which she has to be plucked, howling, and threatened with bludgeoning if she tries it again.

After my divorce she starts spending her summers at the ranch, training a 4-H colt under my father's testy direction. Is she trying to reprise a part of my life? Too late for that, too much has changed. My father has never forgiven me for my defection from the ranch, and this small granddaughter reminds him too much of me for him ever to be gentle with her. He demands more and more of her—longer rides, wetter saddle blankets, blue ribbons, championship trophies—but withholds his praise. *Try harder* is the message she gets.

To this day she keeps an old snapshot of my father on the front of her refrigerator, the one where he poses with Pet, the big-boned sorrel mare with the blaze face and the sweet temper who nearly died in the sleeping-sickness epidemic of the 1930s. In the snapshot Pet's rein is over my father's arm, and she is saddled, humped with cold and furry with winter hair, and he is young and grinning, proud of his snuffy saddle horse.

He never told stories about horses to Elizabeth.

"Pardner? Baby? Old Bauley? Star and Dixie? Socks and Babe?" She shakes her head. "I never heard those names from him."

After a year of living with her father and his new wife in Helena, she asks if she can move back to Havre and live with me again. She says she misses her friends, who have all started their second year at Havre High School without her.

All right, I tell her, but I feel pretty tentative. She has grown a foot, or so it seems, since she has been away, though she is still as slim and wavery as a wand. I hardly know her. I don't trust her at all. Any ill-considered words of mine are likely to be carried down to Helena and then carried back, complete with inflammatory commentary, whereupon I will explode in anger and set off another, worsening cycle. So I will try for no ill-considered words.

Our distance comes to seem normal. Maybe we even forget it's there. She gets A's in high school, avoids getting arrested for anything, otherwise pretty much comes and goes as she pleases. I'm busy, have a lot else on my mind, don't pay much attention. When she goes to work for a local veterinarian, I enjoy the stories she brings home as she works her way up from cleaning cages and carrying food and water and disposing of the stiffened corpses of animals to the more skilled responsibilities of administering shots and assisting with surgery. The jokes that circulate through the veterinary clinic are the best—worst, really—in town; they keep us in stitches. The only one I remember now is the one that asks, Do you know what a delusion of grandeur is? A gnat with a hard-on, lying on his back on a raft in the river, yelling, *Raise the drawbridge!*

In her senior year she spends longer nights with her friends than she does days in school. Girls I've known since they were second-graders drift through the house in a daze, hardly recognizing me, caught in the delusion that only this last year of their lives exists, that high-school graduation will alter them so unimaginably that only this soap-bubble time is real. I know about the keggers out at Beaver Creek Park, of course; everybody knows that free beer flows in the dark for the seniors all night, every night. The kids pass the hat for another keg or they get one of the local business-men to spring for one. Nobody thinks anything about it, Havre's a hard-drinking town. After all, it's only beer; at least Havre kids aren't on drugs!

On this particular night it's past twelve and I've gone to bed when I hear voices, Elizabeth and my husband are talking in the kitchen. Then he opens the bedroom door—"You'd better get up and talk to this kid."

The light doesn't seem to be on, and I don't see her face clearly. She just stands there in the hall, she doesn't make eye contact. Just the monotone of her voice, telling me that she and her friend Celeste were on their way home from tonight's kegger when they rounded a bend in the Beaver Creek Park road and saw, in their headlights, the overturned Cherokee Scout and the four girls who had been headed back to town at high speed to pick a fight with somebody's boyfriend—

God, no.

Dry-eyed, she says their names. Lynn, Sandy, Sarah, Jody— Jody is still alive.

God, no. Not Lynn B——? Not Sandy W——?

Yes. In that inexorable monotone Elizabeth tells the rest of her story. "Sandy was still alive when we got there. She'd been thrown out of the Scout, she was hanging on the fence. I could see"—and for the first time her voice falters—"I never dreamed barbed wire could cut you open like that. I held Sandy's hand. I don't know if she knew I was there. She just kept saying, *I'm sorry,*

I'm sorry. Celeste had called the sheriff on her dad's CB, but for a long time, forever, it was just us there in the dark. After a while Sandy was quiet. I kept holding her hand. Then all at once there were lights, and noise, and all the people in the world were there, and somebody told me to let go of Sandy's hand and go home.''

She doesn't cry. She keeps her arms folded across herself, looks away; and I, caught in my first ignominious reaction—*At least it wasn't my child*—

"Where are you going?" I ask when she sidles away.

"Over to St. Jude's," she says. "A lot of the kids are going to be there."

What I am thinking about, as I watch my daughter disappear from the reach of the streetlight, is the widening distance between us as her experiences soar into a zone of pain beyond any of mine. What will not occur to me, not during the parents' meetings and the guilt, the crackdown on the keggers, and the knowledge that *only by the grace of God it wasn't my child,* what will not occur to me for another ten years, is that not once did I try to touch my daughter that night, nor she to touch me.

So is distance normal, estrangement inevitable? "We're not a family that shows our affection," Auntie told me years ago. "When I drive down to see Ma, she looks up and says, 'I see you got here,' and I say, 'Yes, but the ferry was late,' as though I'd been gone half an hour instead of two or three months. Some people might think we're a little cold."

/ / /

In the fall Elizabeth goes off to Montana State University as a pre-veterinary student. The problem is, men start happening to her. Auntie and I hold our breaths, neither of us daring to say a word, when she gets engaged to an individual whose fraternity brothers call him Thumper. Finally she breaks the engagement, but micro-biology is a casualty. Getting accepted into vet school looms more and more insurmountable for her. Three hundred miles away, in Havre, I wonder what happened to the fearless child, but she comes home less and less frequently.

She's met an engineering student, for one thing, a real Montana boy, like her father. And my home is not a place anyone wants to be. Rachel's father has just been diagnosed with pulmonary fibrosis. Dying, denying that he is dying, he has spiraled our mar-riage into a black carnival of night horrors and unhinged anger with his antic dance with mortality. Rachel is only a year old, and I can deal with little else.

Elizabeth refuses to watch the black carnival. She decides to get married in Bozeman, close to her university friends and to her fiancé's family. But will I sew her wedding dress?

I will. I buy white slipper satin and skeins of white floss. All that spring, in the early mornings, before I go to work, I will sip coffee in the first sunlight while the folds of white satin spill off my lap. Plying my needle, letting my thoughts wander, I hand-embroider sleeves, bodice, hem with heavy white satin-stitch roses, on a dress she will not even come home to try on.

My daughter plans to change her major to zoology and pick up her teaching credentials. After graduation she will go to live in a small town in southern Idaho, where her fiancé already has a good job near some of the best elk-hunting and trout-fishing in the world. He'll fill out his hunting license every year and drink with his buddies in the little jukebox bars in places like St. Anthony and Ashton and bring home most of his paychecks. She might do some substitute-teaching. She'll settle down.

Sure she will.

So now here we both are, Elizabeth and I, farther to the west than we have ever lived, with our backs to the Continental Divide and our faces turned to the confluence of rivers where the Snake opens out into its roll to the Columbia and the Pacific. And I speak the truth to her, for once—"A new baby. I'm so glad"—and by some miracle the truth is the right thing to speak.

By the next day, Elizabeth is explaining to Brian that nobody is ever ready for a baby. Of course she won't give up vet school. With a good baby-sitter and support from Brian she'll manage both.

In May of 1991 she is accepted into the vet med program at Washington State University. And, as Elizabeth will tell the story later to friends, in August the baby pops out, and she says, "Here, Brian, catch," and rushes off to class.

November 1991. Mann's Lake, Idaho. From the rim of the mud bowl, in the chill as the sun dips, I watch the ducks trail their shallow wakes across the surface of the water and think about Imogene's diaries and the secrets she could never tell anyone, and about the secrets I can never tell Elizabeth.

Why has Pete Daniels been on my mind after all these years? Is it a fluke of associations from Imogene's diaries and her revelations about Lud Lind, and the way his name surfaced in her dementia, that is rousing these images for me? A silhouette. Shoulders like a buffalo's. Arms and hands and cock. Flesh I loved in a way I never loved again.

What the rest say about him makes no difference to me, wrote Imogene about Lud in one of the rare bursts of pure pain she allowed herself in nearly fifty years of diaries. *He can't lie or steal faster than those who have never been caught.*

Pete Daniels wasn't a liar or a thief. He was—what? A contained explosion. Rage he couldn't release. In some ways I hardly remember him, know I'm idealizing him. He was just a boy who was married to someone else, and I was married to someone else, and we coupled a few times, briefly and in pain. I should have known better, should have forgotten. I think I must have burned his letters. I've looked for them and can't find them.

9

/ / /

In June of 1991 Elizabeth trailered her horses up from southern Idaho and rented a pasture for them on the bluff above Lewiston, near the airport. Rachel and I went up to watch the mares back out of the horse trailer and snort at their new surroundings, the deep summer grass, the strange sounds and smells of Orchards traffic, and the curious faces of the neighbor's donkeys looking through the fence.

One of these horses is mine, in point of fact. Rijule. A small bay Arabian, absolutely gentle. I bought her for Elizabeth for a 4-H colt, years ago, and now I think that perhaps Rachel can learn to ride her.

The two sorrel mares are a different story. Kip, the younger, has never been fully broken, and though she's got potential, she also is eight years old and running out of time. As for the twelve-year-old mare, she was a filly my father bred back in Montana, out of some crazy thoroughbred stock he picked up somewhere. All that line has been jittery, undependable, and this mare is the one that threw herself into a ditch with Elizabeth a couple years ago and broke her foot. Brian and I call her the Hellbitch, and I wish Elizabeth would get rid of her. It's not worth the price of pasture and hay to keep a horse you can never trust.

Not that I haven't ridden the Hellbitch myself. *That was brave of you,* said my sister, cynically, when she heard about it. I knew I was taking my life in my hands. The Hellbitch will spook at anything. A pheasant rattles up out of the grass ahead of her hoofs, beating its wings and squawking hysterically—*Kwawk, kwawk, this is the worst thing that ever happened to a pheasant*—and the Hellbitch comes undone, or tries to. Leaps about fifteen feet sideways, snorting and trying to get the bit in her teeth. I'm pulling her head around almost to my lap to keep her from stampeding, which is a favorite reaction of hers, and, so thwarted, she lunges to the left, toward a six-foot drop-off she knows is there, and she doesn't even care, she'll throw herself over the edge before she'll stop. I'm swearing at her, kicking the hell out of her with my boot heels, wishing to God I were wearing spurs, and gauging just when I've got to bail off her high side and let her go over that damned bank by herself. Then, just short of disaster, she halts, heavily lathered on her neck and flanks, shaking and breathing hard.

She's ready to behave now. But, damn her, she can never be trusted. She'll spook at the end of a hard ride just as suddenly as she will at the beginning. Ride her hard all summer, and she'll still be spooking in the fall. One of these days she's going to catch one of us unawares, or our luck will just be bad, and she'll get somebody killed.

But Elizabeth loves the Hellbitch. The truth is, the mare is a tie with her grandfather, though I hate to think what he'd have to say about her.

And at least Elizabeth is too heavily pregnant to be riding the Hellbitch this summer. The neighbors never quite get used to the sight of her in maternity jeans and a baggy shirt, lunging one of the mares or trimming their hoofs. The retired veterinarian she used to work for comes out on his deck and shouts at her: "Quit that! Leave that for somebody else to do!"

Rachel is eager to ride. But she doesn't know the first thing. When I saddle Rijule for her, she tries to get on the wrong side, and I can imagine my father turning in his grave. In fact, this corral in the midst of affluent lawns and zinnia beds seems unreal to me, like a bad overlay between me and what I remember. The old smells of horsehair and horse manure only deepen my sense of dissociation. I watch as Rachel lifts the reins tentatively. She grips the saddle horn so tightly that her fingers whiten when Rijule steps out. Over in the shade of trees the Hellbitch switches at flies, as deceptively drowsy as though she wouldn't be off and dancing if somebody came after her with a halter. I think of all the spoiled horses I've ridden in my life. Time was when I almost specialized in spoiled horses, when I rode all the jugheads nobody else wanted to ride. I've never been seriously hurt by a horse—led a charmed life, I guess. But, then, I quit riding when I was seventeen.

Now here I am with these daughters, and these horses that don't know the first thing, either. I've finally realized that a trail horse is one that follows a trail, bored and heavy to rein, when I expect a horse to be alert, responsive, to use its head. To have a purpose in life. To have cattle sense, for example. Like Buck or old Pardner or Paint. Or Dolly.

/ / /

Montana today is overinvented. Tourists drive at eighty miles an hour on Highway 2 across the windswept north face of the state to put the prairie behind them on their way to Glacier National Park, or else they spend a civilized night in Billings and follow Interstate 90 to the south, where they see glamorous Montana, the Big Sky country, where the shadows of clouds drift over the mountains and the trout streams galore, where kids flock from all over the United States to backpack and ski and study creative writing, where movie stars buy ranches and songwriters brim over into rubato:

> *Set me down*
> *Somewhere in the middle of Montana. . . .*

The middle of Montana, its exact geographical center, is Lewistown, in Fergus County, where the fairgrounds Uncle Theo helped to lay out are still ringed with lilacs around the racetrack, where part of the old grandstand still stands, and so does the old horticulture building, where Uncle Theo once exhibited his prize gladioli and his gooseberries. This place has never been glamorous.

I can understand the current tendency to idealize agrarianism and the rural community. I can understand nostalgia for the way life ought to have been. But what I remember is a way of life that it was getting harder and harder to pretend was sustaining.

Lewistown today is slow traffic. It is grain trucks, dusty American-made automobiles, and the Senior Citizens van waiting at one of four or five stoplights on Main Street. With its railroad tracks pried up and its depots closed, its air service dependent upon the weather, and even its bus service inconvenient, it drowses a hundred miles from anywhere, hardly aware that the rest of Montana has become fashionable. Its cattywampus streets are shaded by cottonwoods in summer and clogged by the notorious deep snow of the Judith Basin in the winter. Business has slowed with the decline of farming and ranching, and Lewistown's population of about six thousand grows grayer every year as its young men and women leave Montana in search of work.

When I left home, it was a serious economic blow to my family. They had been counting on me to come back from college after a year or two with a teaching certificate and help support the ranch. I was looking for intellectual challenge? It wouldn't have been a concept my father understood. The very notion would have angered him, as did so much else. He allowed little margin in his world for deviance.

"How Father would have hated that dog," my sister remarks about my foolish mutt, Bear. And certainly I know Bear is useless, with his terrier's whiskers and his yap, although he sleeps on my bed and lies under my desk while I write.

And yet, like Imogene, I am drawn back almost every summer. I drive Highway 12 out of Idaho, over Lolo Pass, and then I drop down the Montana side of the pass to Missoula and take I-90 to Deer Lodge, where an old friend always takes me in and gives me a bed in a cool room with drawn shades in the house where she has lived, off and on, since childhood. She and I talk, in the private coded language of two women who have known each other, and most of each other's secrets, for twenty years, while Rachel, if she is with me, gets bored and goes to swing at the school playground across the street.

In the morning we drive over another mountain pass—
McDonald Pass, this time—and then drop down into Helena, and
then through Wolf Creek Canyon to Great Falls, where we cut
across on Highway 87 to Lewistown. We have come only about
five hundred miles. The last forty miles, I start pointing out the
missing landmarks to Rachel, as if she cares.

See? That was our road, that's where our mailbox was.

Why did I have to make a choice between going home and being
slowly suffocated, and having to break ties with home to breathe
my own air? Why were the smallest betrayals enough to bring on
one of my father's icy silences, and why did I have to guess what
I'd done wrong? Why did I have to stop riding horses, and how
can I ever reconnect the first seventeen years of my life with the
present?

I remember Yellow Wolf, who, when Colonel Gibbon attacked
the Nez Percés on the Montana side of the territorial line, was
twenty-two years old. After fighting the troopers, Yellow Wolf
rode back into the Big Hole and saw the dead in the Nez Percé
camp: *This tepee here was standing and silent. Inside we found the two
women lying in their blankets dead. Both had been shot. The mother had
her newborn baby in her arms. Its head was smashed, as by a gun breech
or boot heel.*

The surviving Nez Percés fled east, then north, hoping to escape
across the Canadian line, where the Sioux already had taken sanc-
tuary after their defeat of Custer at the battle of the Little Big
Horn. By September of 1877 the Nez Percés had reached the
Judith Basin, right here in sight of these mountains, where they
surprised and killed several of a Crow hunting party and took their
horses and their fresh buffalo meat. Then they continued north,

crossing the Missouri River at Cow Island, where Yellow Wolf and other young warriors raided a steamboat supply depot and killed a trooper and several teamsters. Somewhere near the Milk River they met a party of half-breeds traveling south, and one of the half-breed women remembered all her life how sorry she felt for the little Nez Percé children.

As everyone knows, the Nez Percés never reached Canada. General Miles caught them in their last camp in the shadow of the Bear's Paw Mountains and pinned them down with artillery. Yellow Wolf thought of home: *Then with rifle I stood forth, saying to my heart, 'Here I will die, fighting for my people and our homes.'* But Yellow Wolf didn't die at the Bear's Paw. He lived to be seventy-nine years old, and he never spoke of his first twenty-two years but once, and not even to his own sons, but to an insistent white friend, L. V. McWhorter, who wrote it all down.

So these landmarks of old hunting grounds, the high blue line of the Snowies and the faraway haze of the Bear's Paw Mountains, must have been almost as familiar to some of the Nez Percés as they are to me, or as they became to my great-grandfather, who arrived in Montana in 1882 as a surveyor with the Northern Pacific Railroad and stayed to prove up on a dryland claim and raise sheep in the Judith Basin.

This country was empty when we came to it, we were all told. In 1882 my great-grandfather would have heard that Sitting Bull had come back from Canada and surrendered the year before, and he may have known that the surviving Nez Percés had been shipped to exile in Oklahoma, as had the Northern Cheyennes, and he may have known that the Blackfeet were starving on their reservation in the north. It was a great deal of knowledge to have to suppress or justify. In one of the undated diary entries he kept on scrap paper, my great-grandfather notes his encounter with a little band of Piegans on the old Carroll Trail. Fortunately, he remarks, the Piegans had just gorged themselves on buffalo, so they were not begging:

> *Then away they drift, these conquerors of the coyote and wolf, alternately gorging and starving, against whom the white man has 'sinned' in killing off the buffalo thus removing their 'feast without effort.'*

So, when Imogene or I try to reconnect by coming back to our roots, what we find is a story that has been rewritten. In fact, a whole alternate history.

> *. . . in the spring of 1879 a band of twenty-five families headed by Pierre Berger started from the Milk River. . . . Somehow we got through safely to the mouth of Spring Creek, around the Judith Mountains and to the north of them, came in by way of the gap to the famous Judith Basin, which was indeed a paradise land of plenty, game of all kinds, lots of good water and timber. What more could we want? After finding what we had searched for, our journey ended right here.*

The speaker is the half-breed woman who remembered how sorry she felt for the little Nez Percé children. Her name is Clemence Berger, and she was the daughter-in-law of old Pierre. She is describing what her people later called the Long Journey, when those twenty-five families of Métis, or Red River half-breeds, had left Turtle Mountain and come down to central Montana to start a settlement which (granted enough imagination and faith in the improbable) might have become not an obscure Montana ranch town named Lewistown but the capital city of a native nation called Assiniboia (always supposing the Riel Rebellion against the Canadian government in 1885 had been successful instead of a bloodily suppressed uprising of "savage Catholic breeds").

Clemence again: *While we roamed the prairies of western Minnesota and the Dakotas, we were always in the company of people of part-Indian blood . . . just camping here and there without thought of settling permanently in any place, just following the buffalo trails. You might think that we lived the life of real Indians, but one thing we had always with us which they did not—religion. Wherever we were we had some Jesuit missionaries along.*

The half-breeds danced to fiddle music, and they followed the buffalo in Red River carts, which were made entirely of wood lashed together with rawhide and drawn by a single pony or ox. According to the historian Joseph Kinsey Howard, the wooden wheels sounded, when turning on their ungreased wooden axles, "as if a thousand fingernails were drawn across a thousand panes of glass." It was in these screeching Red River carts, in a long slow-rising column of dust, that Clemence's father-in-law led his twenty-five families down from the Milk River to Spring Creek in 1879. The old man had correctly foreseen the end of the buffalo culture for Indians and breeds alike. What they needed now, Pierre told the others, was a safe place where they could build cabins and plant gardens.

Pierre sounds a lot like my great-uncle Theo.

/ / /

And so the history of this place is a hundred-year-old repressed memory. One story can be narrated only by denying another.

This place was empty when we came here, they told us. But Imogene and I were born here, we didn't know about emptiness. We could not hear the silence, because we had never heard city noise. What we heard was wind, ragging constantly at grass and sagebrush, and what we saw were shadows of giant drifting clouds and two ruts of road leading to a distant point. The dry hills outlining our horizons were the shapes of our own bodies.

We might have gone on living where narrow trails were shaped like the soles of our feet and landmarks loomed like the edges of conscious thought. But the land died under us. In the drought years, even the creeks stopped running. Our blood stopped. *Hang on,* said our parents. But we had years to spin out between the parched prairie of our births and the waterless cemetery ridge where twenty years were enough to bleach the names and dates off the slabs of planks at the heads of graves. We had to try for another narrative.

The worst thing I have been able to uncover about Lud Lind is that he was a Catholic and he was a Bohunk, which was the label used indiscriminately by their white Protestant neighbors for any of the first-generation Central European emigrants. Bohemians, Czechoslovakians, Croatians, everyone knows they're all alike. They talk their old-country talk at home, and they practice their filthy habits, and they have ten, eleven kids to a family, they go at it worse than animals, and then they don't believe in educating the kids, they put them right to work. Only thing worse for a decent white ranch girl than going out with a Bohunk would be going out with one of the breeds.

The photograph Elizabeth and I found in the box of Imogene's unsorted pictures shows Lud with his hat tilted back from his face, holding a struggling blaze-faced foal—"A workhorse foal," Elizabeth thinks. The tension in his pose still vibrates after sixty years.

"What do you think happened to him?" Elizabeth asks.

"Oh, he died. Eventually." Alone, in fact, in 1975. I've seen his obituary. *After a long illness.* He was sixty-three.

Elizabeth contributes a memory of her own. "Do you know that I saw his letters to her once? They were in a bundle in a box in the attic of the old homestead house. I was just a little kid. They were all signed *Lud, XXX OOO,* and I wondered what that meant."

Hugs and kisses, dummy, somebody told her. Now, leave those letters be. They're not yours.

I had rarely heard Imogene speak his name until recently, when some peculiar reflexive action of the brain as it started closing in on itself seemed to bring him back to the surface. Trying to stay in contact with her inner ramblings, I sorted out her diaries for the 1930s, when Lud seemed to have dropped out of Imogene's life, and started reading for clues. I cared less about Lud and what had happened to him than I did about whatever had led Imogene to close a certain door behind her. In some ways, Lud himself seemed too pat an answer. I didn't believe in the lost-sweetheart theory any more than I did in the significance of coinciding dreams.

Summer of 1935. The dirty thirties. Lud owns the clothes he stands up in. He has less than eight years of schooling. One of eleven children—*They're Bohunks, after all*—he can hope for nothing from his father's blighted homestead. In fact, he will work at unskilled jobs for most of his life.

What would Imogene's life have been like if she had married Lud? Unimaginable. But for a few weeks during the summer of 1935, knowing nothing of the faceless years ahead, Lud and Imogene shared a brief suspension from time, riding horseback together along the breaks and slapping mosquitoes and swimming in the sparse shade of willows hanging over the deep holes in the Judith River.

Monday, July 29, 1935. Lud asked me to go swimming after supper. . . . Was Dad sore. . . .

Friday, August 2, 1935. Lud fixed the tires. He talked about every important subject.

No story is ever the whole story. When I was a child I sometimes listened to the women's bitten-off conversations. Always they talked while they were working, shelling peas together, perhaps, on the porch in the heat of the day.

My grandmother's hands were shaped like mine, with strong tendons that rose out of the fine brown excess of her wrinkled skin when she snapped open a pod and shucked the peas rattling into the pan on her lap—Bennett hands, she called them. I can still see their smooth unconscious motion. Toss the empty pod into one milk pail, reach for a full pod from the other milk pail, snap and shuck and toss and reach for another. And here comes my other grandmother, plodding up from the garden in the full sun with a pailful of unshelled peas in either hand.

"I tore a little with Kathryn," Grandma is saying. What can she mean?

My mother's voice rises with the irritation of the generation that knows better than the last. "The doctor won't let you tear nowadays, he'll cut—"

"A tear is more natural."

Grandma says about my mother, "Doris was the easiest of all my babies. I went to Great Falls to have Imogene and Kathryn, but I had a woman come out to the homestead when Doris was born, and that was the easiest time I had."

My other grandmother will set down her bucket of peas and add her one childbirth story, how her water broke before she could get to Lewistown and therefore my father was born in his grand-father's log ranch house on Spring Creek. But Imogene is never a part of these cryptic confidences in the scent of raw green peapods. She has never married, never had a child, can neither give nor receive these small secrets.

"Why do you think she never married?" asks Elizabeth.

Some people just aren't meant to get married, my mother used to say. *In our family there's an old maid in every generation. There's Aunt Mable and now there's Imogene.*

And certainly there was always about Imogene, as I remember her, a kind of indifference. Numbness, I wonder now?

Maybe. But she never did a thing she didn't want to do, never did anything merely to make a show or an impression. I have a snapshot of her at age four, standing on the front steps of the homestead shack with her sisters and her father, who leans back in a rocking chair with baby Doris, my mother, on his lap. He is smiling, proud of all his little girls. Little Kathryn has not yet died and wiped all the smiles off his face. Kathryn stands at his knee, Sylva tilts toward him with an elfin smile. But Imogene stands squarely with her feet apart and her stomach thrust out, the same uncompromising posture at age four as she has at eighty. No one who ever saw her standing in front of her house in Idaho with her feet spread apart and her dog under her arm could ever mistake that jut of her head, that unreadable stare.

When Imogene was five she refused to let her mother teach her to read from a primer as she had Sylva. Finally she had to be tricked into learning to read. Every evening, while they washed the supper dishes, her mother and Sylva talked over the stories they had been reading in *The Youth's Companion,* stories they refused to read aloud to her. Tantalized, Imogene finally had to buckle down and learn to read the stories for herself.

And Imogene won't learn to tie her shoes, won't learn which is her left foot and which her right, gets her shoes on the correct feet only about half the time, and this after she is old enough to hitch a horse to the buggy and drive all the way into Denton by herself to meet Aunt Mable at the railroad station—"I drove past some kids in town, and they laughed and pointed at me, so I knew I had my shoes on the wrong feet again, so I drove around a corner and switched them," she told me.

Imogene shows Aunt Mable all over the homestead, climbs the rimrocks with her, teaches her how to drive the old white mare down the rutted road through the sage, and how to draw a bead with the .22 rifle and squeeze the trigger. What a pair they are, that lanky Iowa schoolteacher and that tough little Montana-born girl! In their excitement they almost murder the white mare one afternoon. Imogene, showing off for Aunt Mable, fires at a gopher from the buggy without thinking and is horrified when her shot parts the mare's mane. Used to them, unaware of her close call, the mare only flinches and shakes her head.

"Could she have been gay?" Elizabeth asks.

I try to see through the know-it-all labels of the late twentieth century to Imogene as I remember her. No. I don't think so. It was more as though she'd never gone through puberty, never felt the stir—although she was always curious—

Or is it Aunt Mable I'm thinking about?

Mable was my grandmother's youngest sister, and she was useful to her family as an unmarried woman. She took care of an old uncle until he died, and then she took care of her father until he died. Then she went on teaching kindergarten in Iowa until she retired and went out to Seattle to live the rest of her days with my grandmother on the farm.

She was white-haired and innocent when I first remember her, but still she went out to the woodpile and sorted out the lumber to hammer together a pair of stilts for me so she could teach me to walk on them. Yes, her blue eyes, her curiosity! I could hardly believe a grown-up could be such a playmate. Being a child was what she knew; she rambled happily with me just as she had with Imogene when Imogene was my age, just as, in her eighties, she would drop down cross-legged on the floor to play jacks or Chinese checkers with my children.

She always retained her child's tender heart. Later on the same afternoon when Imogene nearly shot the white mare, Aunt Mable took her turn with the .22 rifle and blithely blazed away at a meadowlark on a fence post—and was horrified to see it topple over dead. Perhaps it only fainted from fear, she told Imogene, and it would revive after they drove away.

Aunt Mable was curious about sex, but she had to resort to the unmarried woman's devious ways of finding out what she wanted to know. She confided in Imogene, and Imogene in me, about the time when, driving alone through Wyoming on the long empty stretch of highway between Buffalo and Gillette, Aunt Mable happened to see two horses copulating in a fence corner. On that flat prairie she could see the road for miles ahead of her and behind her. She could not possibly be taken unawares by another car. So she turned around and drove back to where she could pull off on the side of the road in the scent of sweet clover and watch to her heart's content while the great horses arched and rocked and throbbed into each other.

The more obvious it was that Mable would never marry, the better her family liked it. How useful she was! They borrowed money from her, borrowed her car, came to depend on her. In return all she asked was to live on the edges of her sisters' families, to love their children. What in the world would her nieces and nephews have done if she had married and had children of her own? If they had had no Aunt Mable?

What if I had had no Imogene?

In March of 1991 I was getting ready to fly to Wyoming for a week's residency when an aide from the Villa Villekula telephoned in a high state of excitement: "Your aunt's lost a tooth! A gold tooth! She came carrying it to us in her hand! We've saved the tooth, but she needs to see a dentist right away!''

"All right," I said, "I'll see what I can do."

Why now? But several phone calls later not only had I gotten my aunt an emergency appointment with the dentist, but I had persuaded the Villekula staff to get her there so I could finish packing and escape to the airport.

"And tell them not to lose that tooth!" the dentist's receptionist had warned. "They're terrible! They lost my mother's wheelchair! A whole wheelchair! They can lose anything!"

So, when I get back from Wyoming, I am pleased to learn that the Villekula staff did get Auntie to the dentist on time, and also that they remembered to bring along the gold crown. The only problem is, the stub of her tooth under the crown was rotten, so the dentist pulled it. Now Auntie doesn't need the crown. But they have saved it for me.

All this I learn from the dentist's receptionist when I bring Auntie back to the dentist for her regular checkup the week after I get home from Wyoming. I appreciate the dentist's receptionist. She has, as she says, "been through it" with her mother, who suffered from Alzheimer's disease. She is one of the few people who really see me when I creep through the waiting-room door at Auntie's pace, balancing her on my arm. Others glance up from their magazines and hardly bother to glance away, as I have so often glanced away from the middle-aged woman with the tottery old lady on her arm in the doctor's office, the dentist's office, the Office of Social Security. I'm not invisible, it's just that nobody sees me.

"Here's your gold crown!" says the receptionist, triumphantly handing me an envelope with something weighty in one corner. I look quickly inside and shut the envelope again. The crown looks just like a gold molar, all right.

"I'm so glad they remembered it," I tell the receptionist, "but what am I supposed to do with it now?"

She looks shocked. "It belongs to you. It's valuable!"

"I suppose it is, but what do you do with a tooth?"

"Well—for example, you might want to take it to a jeweler and have it melted down. You could have an earring made. Or a gold charm for a charm bracelet."

"Or," says one of the hygienists, "you could save up until you have enough gold teeth, and have them made into a really nice piece of jewelry."

My aunt listens with little show of interest. She didn't want to come to the dentist today. She can't remember what she had for lunch, but she does know that she has been to the dentist very recently, and she doesn't want to do it again. Having a tooth pulled probably does tend to linger in the memory.

But now, as I stuff the tooth envelope into a pocket and guide my aunt to a chair and sit down beside her, I see that she has undergone a change of mood.

Usually when my aunt cries, it is because she is old and helpless and can't do what she wants to do. Or it's the medication, I have been told. Or it's the aftereffect of a stroke that triggers the tears, which means that her weeping has nothing to do with her emotional state. But I don't know. It seems to me that she has plenty to cry about.

Her money, she worries. Is her money safe in the bank?

"Yes," I tell her.

Her will. What about her will?

I reassure her, explain to her all over again what her will says, promise her that I will carry out all her bequests.

"Oh, oh, oh!" she sobs. "You do so much for me! I've asked you to do so much."

After the months of listening to her recriminations, I hardly know how to handle her contrition.

"I've been reading your diaries," I tell her, to change the subject. "Is it all right with you if I read your diaries?"

"You can have all my writings," she says instantly.

"You had a horse named Dolly, once. Was Dolly a gray?"

"No." Her eyes go filmy, searching inwardly. "She was a bay."

A bright bay, confirms my mother in a letter a few weeks from now.

"Do you remember how you used to ride Dolly down to the spring and fetch back water in buckets? And sometimes she would buck you off, water and all?"

"No," she says. But after another long moment, as though fumbling through the dark reaches, she retrieves another fragment. "After I'd filled my buckets, I used to set them on a fence post so I could get on Dolly and then pick them up."

Before I can marvel at the magic of memory, at the power of the precious trivial, she bursts into tears again. "Oh, oh, oh! I'm so afraid that I'm going to die, and then you will be left all alone."

So, Imogene, did you ever dream about Lud?

Early in February I had dreamed about the man called Pete Daniels, whom I had known in northern Montana, where it always seems to be arctic daylight. But in my dream the air seemed dark and heavy and still. Although I had not in fact spoken to Pete Daniels in nearly twenty years, in my dream he and I were talking to each other across an enormous empty parking lot, which I gradually recognized as the parking lot behind the emergency entrance of St. Joseph's Hospital. The floodlights erased shadows and blotted out the stars, like a concrete nightmare of the next century. I could hear Pete Daniels's voice across that bowl of concrete and electric light, but I could not see his face, for he stood at the base of one of the light towers, far away as a stick figure, and I stood alone on my side of the pavement, where the shrubbery had been flattened into cutouts. And I woke up disturbed, trying to retrieve the shreds on both ends of the dream.

I was in Boise a few weeks later for a state-committee meeting when a man I knew from another university stopped me in the hotel lobby and said, "Hello from Pete Daniels—we interviewed him on our campus at the first of February."

10

/ / /

Lately, Imogene, I've had trouble concentrating on your story. I've got one of my own that's clamoring for my attention, and the worst of it is, I can't tell it to anyone else, though God knows I've been on the verge of telling it to you. It's the ambience of the Villa Villekula that defeats me. Can you imagine me, sitting beside you in one of those plastic-covered armchairs and, in between your sobs and your worries about your bank account, within earshot of the blah-blah woman and the crawling man and the old gobber and the rest of that poor addled old crew, telling you all about my failed romance of twenty years ago?

On the other hand, maybe the Villa Villekula is the place to tell that story. I feel that foolish about it. I'm not young, I'm sober most of the time, so why am I mooning through the daylight hours and dreaming at night? I have the feeling that I could stop the images, if I only would; but the truth is, there's a pleasure, a lure, an indulgence, that I want to sink back into. Harmless, I try to tell myself. Harmless to catch myself with my eyes vaguely fixed on nothing, to realize an hour has slipped away, to slide back into awareness of Rachel's insistent "Mom! Mom!" as she tries to regain my attention.

Who is Pete Daniels? Let's say he's a cowboy, let's say he's the kind who owns his saddle and the clothes he stands up in, and let's also say he drifts around the West, now here, now there, working on one of the few remaining ranches that run cattle the way they used to. Or maybe Pete Daniels follows the rodeo circuit. You might spot his name in the local paper, on the premium list for the saddle-bronc riding, or, then again, you might see it in the police reports for drunkenness or assault.

Or let's say Pete Daniels tends bar somewhere in the West, maybe in one of those little towns along the Montana highline that has a couple of grain elevators and a store and a bowling alley, a town that used to have a railroad depot and still has its name in black letters on a white board that faces the rail bed where tall grass blows endlessly and the gravel streets get narrower every year. Winter or summer, the sun exposes the cracks and splinters in the false fronts, but in the Palace Bar or the Montana Club or the Hackamore it will be dark even at two in the afternoon, and the good old boys sit at the bar in their caps and watch themselves in the mirror as they suck their beers. They like Pete Daniels even if he is a breed kid from Fort Belknap with a few too many tailfeathers left from his fights with the toughs and the would-be toughs on and off the reservation.

Pete Daniels won't stay long at the Hackamore Bar. He'll turn up here, there. In the Dakotas, maybe. As far east as St. Paul. Or out on the West Coast for a while. He leaves his wife, goes back to her, leaves her again. *Women love him half to death,* sings Emmylou. It's the sound of his laugh, it's his easy ways, it's his dark face and the violence he radiates. What's wrong with him? Is it his rage turned inward? Is that why he can't look back?

Hardly seems to matter. Where Pete Daniels is headed is all too predictable. Alcohol, car wrecks, gunshots—life expectancy for young men from the Fort Belknap Reservation is about thirty-five years.

So what is Pete Daniels doing in graduate school? Why is he interviewing in English departments? What happened to the narrative?

It may be that the disintegration of the brain is a mechanical process, a whirring of broken film on a spool that throws one image after another on a screen in split-second random flashes. Can one flash matter more than another? The bay horse Dolly, the spilled water, the name of the man? Continuity has been disrupted, arrangement seems accidental. With the absence of any sustaining narrative, with the loss of the story by which my aunt constructed herself and assigned a shape to her life, those ragtag-and-bobtail fragments retain only the meaning that I might impose upon them.

And yet I keep looking for clues.

Imogene, your diary entry for Friday, March 15, 1935, is the first I can find that might refer to Lud. In March of 1935 you are twenty-four years old and enrolled for the winter term at the University of Minnesota and worrying about your grades and your finances. You are flunking calculus, doing badly in U.S. history. Aunt Mable sends money and advice. But you are homesick. You live for letters from home, note in your diary the ones you send and the ones you receive—

Letter from my old friend the horsethief. Could kick his pants.

"Oh, yes! That's Lud!" said my mother when I showed her the entry.

Is it? Imogene doesn't mention Lud by name until June of 1935, and then in the accidental way that so many of the characters in her diaries briefly swim to the surface only to sink back into oblivion. By June of 1935 she has left the University of Minnesota, having flunked out in spite of her work and tears—*made a regular fizzel of calculus,* she reports in one of the agonized entries that make it so difficult for me to reconcile the twenty-four-year-old girl with the woman I knew. She came back to Montana and taught the spring term at a country school, and now she is back on the ranch and living with her parents for the summer. Also living in that close two-room house, and in a foul mood most of the time over the failure of her boyfriend to turn up when she expects him, is Imogene's twenty-one-year-old sister, Doris.

I can't tell from Imogene's diaries whether Lud was working for her father that summer, or whether he just hung around a lot:

Friday, June 14. I helped chase cows for Dad. Boy the first time I rode Lud's mare she gave me a real ride through the corn.

Saturday, June 22. Lud took us to a play & dance in Denton. Doris' boy friend came after we left. Was she on the prod.

As the summer eases into July, Imogene's diary entries gradually reveal a predictable pattern in which Lud is the constant strand.

Thursday, July 4. Doris started a fight last night & today I stole her envelope from Jack. Was she mad. Lud & I rode to the river & got some horsehair for a saddle blanket.

Friday, July 5. Jack took Doris to a dance last night so she should be good natured for a while.

Saturday, July 6. Jack, George & Tiny came & took Doris to a dance. Lud & I went in the Chivie. Lud said he was going to give me D. regardless.

Monday, July 8. Lud cultivated the corn with the duckfoot. I helped him get in his cow & calf. It rained & hailed a little.

Wednesday, July 10. Lud & I rode yesterday afternoon & killed a rattler.

And so on. The trivial, backbreaking chores, the small pleasures, the obscure marginalia. I speculated for a long time over "Lud said he was going to give me D. regardless" until it occurred to me that I was seeing an early reference to the bay mare Dolly (was Dolly the mare that ran through the corn?) that Lud gave to Imogene and then may have stolen back from her.

By the middle of July her entries reveal that all is not well:

Friday, July 12. Lud & the Old Man had a round.

Saturday, July 13. Lud sure gave Dad the st. goods. Told him he'd milk the cow if he wanted to leave.

Sunday, July 14. Went to Hoosac & was Dad sore. I was sick all day—heat & nerves I guess.

Nerves? Imogene? Whatever happened to the tough ten-year-old who once beat up on every kid at the Baulley Dome School on a single afternoon?

It had started with a fight over a gopher trap, as she told the story to me. There was one eighth-grade boy in the Baulley Dome School, named Tom, and he had promised Imogene she could play with his gopher trap at recess. Then he promised another fourth-grade girl that *she* could play with it. Tom had done this deliberately, Imogene said, to set the little girls against each other and see what would happen. Imogene grabbed the gopher trap away from the other little girl and swung it around her head, scattering the first-graders, and then she punched the other girl in the stomach and sent her off bawling. Before recess was over she had beaten up on everybody but Tom, of course, and her sister Sylva, who always stayed inside the schoolhouse and read a book during recess.

I recognize the tough girl just as I recognize the four-year-old in the snapshot with her stomach thrust out and her face inscrutable. But the vulnerable young woman, caught unawares in her own secret pages, who is she?

By the summer of 1935 Imogene is a round-faced young woman with dark eyes and carefully waved dark hair. She poses with her dog against the sun-blistered siding of the house. Self-conscious, she glances away from the camera. She is overweight and worried about it; her diaries recount her agonized efforts to crash off five pounds in three days, ten pounds in a week. Her dress is a home-made cotton print that looks too tight.

Imogene has another worry. Where will she find a school to teach in the fall? Unwilling to grant tenure, the country school boards rarely keep a teacher long. They pay as little as they can, sometimes a hundred but often seventy, sixty dollars a month, and sometimes, if the district is pinched, they withhold the teacher's warrants altogether. And they take their time hiring. July and August can pass without the teacher's knowing for sure where she'll find a school this fall, how far from town it will be, whether or not the kids will be unruly, or their families suspicious, or whether the water out there at Winnett or Valentine or Cat Creek will be alkaline and undrinkable.

Imogene's mother has been moving from school to school all over the Judith Basin, teaching a year here, two years there, for nearly thirteen years. Somehow she's scraped together enough money from her pay warrants to send all three of her daughters to normal school long enough to get teaching certificates of their own. She has bought them a marginal freedom they're not sure they want. Last September her oldest daughter, Sylva, left teaching to get married and move to Fort Peck with her husband. But Imogene and Doris are just starting out in the life.

Monday, July 15. Went out to Arrowcreek to see about the school. Sure ate a lot of crap.

Monday, July 22. Went over to Arrow Creek but got no results. Said they'd let us know in a week.

Wednesday, July 24. Was asked to take the North Everson school till Xmas. Doris & I went out to see about it. Must decide Sat.

Friday, July 26. Didn't get Arrow Creek. Guess Doris will try to take N. Everson & the Old Man will be sore.

When Sylva got married and moved to Fort Peck, where her young husband had found work on the new dam project, it nearly broke her mother's heart. To give up a hundred-dollar-a-month school to marry a boy nine years younger than herself, a boy without even an eighth-grade education, without money or skills or resources of his own, without even a decent family background—his parents took *bankruptcy!* They went on *relief!* The shame of it, and the dangers of life in wide-open, roaring Fort Peck for her delicate, bookish Sylva, was all her mother could talk about, while her younger daughters listened, and Doris secretly made up her own mind.

Friday, August 9. Doris talks of Jack and I guess Aunt Mable & Ma know what is in her mind. But not how soon.

In fact, Doris will marry Jack the following April. And Imogene is going to dances with Lud Lind—and what is so disturbing, after all, about these modest romances, these thoughts of marriage, on the part of these young women? Sounds normal, even?

It is probably her mother who fuels the tensions in that shack that drive Imogene to sick headaches and nervous exhaustion, although her diary entries tend to blame her father.

True, her father is prey to tantrums and bewildering mood shifts. He's been surly for years, getting worse. After Kathryn died, he never smiled again, never got down on the floor and played with his other little girls, never held them on his lap and read to them, as he used to do. Sometimes he explodes in rages.

Sometimes he withdraws for hours or days into a corner of the kitchen, his eyes gone abstract. Sulking? Daydreaming? The women don't know. They have learned that they cannot count on him. Doris and Imogene and even their mother get Lud or Jack to drive them on their endless summer rounds of the central-Montana counties in search of schools to teach in the fall.

Her own car, Imogene will tell herself, and her diary. *If only she had her own car.*

Imogene's mother had started teaching in Montana in 1922, after the homestead failed. She had to study at night and take an examination at the courthouse in Lewistown to renew her teaching certificate, and then she had to take a country school miles from home. Live in the teacherage during the week with her children, drive for hours by team and wagon on weekends to get back to the ranch and wash clothes and iron and clean and bake for the coming week. But she couldn't count on *him,* and she needed the pay warrant, that was how she kept everybody fed. Now, nearly thirteen years into the grind of rural teaching, seeing another fifteen years of the grind ahead of her, she boils over. Tells him in front of the girls what a spineless piece of incompetence he is, what a disappointment he has been, and what she thinks of his worthless promises of free land in Montana, and a comfortable ranch home, and respectability.

To her daughters she says, *Don't marry.* She did all she could to prevent Sylva's marriage. Now she does her best to delay Doris's plans. Wait another year. Better to stand on your own feet. Don't give up your monthly pay warrant. Don't trust your security to a man.

/ / /

"I never knew Imogene was unhappy," says my mother, close to tears as she puts down the transcript of the diaries. "She always seemed so happy. She was always laughing. Always."

Friday, August 23. Went job hunting with no success. God—where will I be in one month—next year?

Sunday, September 1. Lud & I rode again for the last time this year. Sunday rides have been my bright spots.

Monday, September 2. Big fight on how we go to the teacher's meeting. Doris won, I guess—go by train.

Tuesday, September 3. Well, she lost, Lud came in his Dad's car. He took me to town. . . .

Friday, September 6. Lud came back just to see me. Brot a box of candy. . . .

Saturday, September 7. With no job—Ma hurt me by saying I was poor making money. Doris & she were so much better. Cried softly making my bed.

Sunday, September 8. Got a phone call yesterday—Lud took me here (Roy). Got a six-month for $66—cried after he left.

Monday, September 9. First day of school over—not all here—little kids—queer neighbors—Bohemians. And the water situation!

Tuesday, September 17. Just another day—how time drags. Always before it went flying.

Wednesday, September 18. How slow the clock ticks the time away. . . .

Thursday, September 19. Another day gone . . .

Friday, September 20. Friday at last. Sent the kids home half an hour early. Went home and howled.

"She must have hated teaching," says Elizabeth, laying down the pages. "I never realized. I always supposed she liked to teach."

"It was the only choice she thought she had." I show Elizabeth a few of the diary entries for the following fall, when Imogene did not find a school to teach until far into September:

Friday, September 11, 1936. Went to Lewistown—stopped at the laundry—they only pay 20¢ an hour. . . .

Monday, September 14, 1936. Mon & I can't go to the teacher's meeting. No news of a job . . .

Monday, September 21, 1936. Mrs. Sterrit called me up—sent me to a school near Winnett. Lud took me after dinner . . . only $65.

During the fall of 1935 and the winter of 1936, Imogene puts in long days at the Roy School, notes the weather, her weariness, her letters from her family. *No mail from Doris at all. Darn her.*

She is only about sixty miles from home, but it might as well be six hundred miles, over gravel roads and dirt ruts and, through much of the winter, blizzards and drifting snow that closes even the highways. No telephone. No radio. Sometimes she waits all weekend, hoping Lud will fight his way through the drifts to spend a few hours with her. Many days she sees no one but her schoolchildren. After they have gone home, she writes letters or reads, if she has a book, or she cuts quilt pieces and sews.

The quilt she's working on this winter is a Stars and Flowers pattern, briefly popular during the thirties. When I was in graduate school, my mother let me trace a pattern from her Stars and Flowers quilt, which she probably pieced about the same time that Imogene was piecing hers, and I, too, in the late evenings or early mornings when I was too tired or too tense to study, learned the solace in the rhythm of a needle, the measuring of time by the length of a thread, and the strength of cotton fabric in my hands.

Gradually the weather breaks and the days lengthen into what passes for spring on the northern plains. Imogene cleans the teacherage, melts snow for water to wash her clothes, scolds the children for playing in the mud. On Saturday, April 4, 1936, she notes only, *School election. Went for my mail and washed blankets,* although on that day, in the Methodist parsonage in faraway Denton, her sister Doris is marrying Jack Hogeland. The handful of wedding guests will pose on the parsonage porch, bundled against the sharp April wind in their coats and overshoes behind the smiling young couple—her mother and father, his widowed mother, his uncle Theo and aunt Em. But not Imogene, she is in Roy, too far away to attend.

But her spirits lift as April thaws the roads and Lud is able to fetch her home for a weekend:

Thursday, April 23. Lud surprised me & came. Roads were bad on the other side of Brooks. I guess the folks miss Doris a lot.

Friday, April 24. We started for the dance—the roads were bad & the axle broke on the Putman hill so we walked home.

Saturday, April 25. The folks were disappointed. I was worried over getting back but Lud said he'd get me there.

Sunday, April 26. The horses came & we finally run them in. So Lud rode Dolly—fixed the car by noon—took Ma & me to our schools—we had a heart to heart talk.

And then finally the end of May, the closing of the Roy School, and home for another summer of chores and uneventful days on the ranch, going to dances and rodeos with Lud, riding horseback through the river breaks to visit the newly married Doris, worrying about where she will find her next school to teach.

Can this life change?

Sunday, June 28. Lud & I went riding. Took out some salt for antelope. He saw 5 this morning. Had a good talk. Found currents, gooseberries, sarvisberries.

When she finally gets the school near Winnett in September of 1936, she settles in for another year of tedium. She learns to crochet from one of the neighbor women, edges a pair of pillow cases in pink and white, and adds them to the little pile of linens in an old trunk she calls her hope chest. Lud comes to see her on a rare Sunday afternoon, later writes that he has a plan. He is trying to get horses to break, trying to raise a little cash money.

Sunday, November 8, 1936. Still no word from Ma. Haven't heard in 2 weeks. Letter from Doris—rather snippy. Told me to make other plans for Xmas.

Monday, November 9, 1936. Rather tired—& very blue from the letters. Doris & Lud must have had a quarrel.

"Is Doris trying to break them up, or what?" Elizabeth wonders.

I don't know. My mother at twenty-two was taller than her sisters, gray-eyed and slim. A beauty, really, with her flashing smile and her energy. Though she didn't know she was beautiful; she had been brought up like her older sisters by the harsh old adages that disallowed personal vanities or even the small pleasures of pretty clothes or any other adornment. Her temper was legendary. She flared up at her father and her sisters, slammed through the homestead shack, fought with her mother.

Imogene's diary entries back in 1935 reflect Doris's growing antagonism toward her and Lud. *Doris & Lud fought & so spoiled some things—Doris got me to break a date to a dance to stay in town so she could see Jack & now I bet she forgets all about taking us to Deerfield next Sat.—Doris wouldn't let me wear her housedress for meanness so Ma said she'd get me one—Doris fights Lud all the time—Doris keeps us all in hot water over Jack.*

Quiet morning—Doris not here, Imogene ends her diary for 1935.

But by the fall of 1936, Doris has got what she wanted. She's married Jack and is living with him and his mother on their ranch, and she loves riding with Jack and working beside him and going with him to the country dances. The years of hard work and hard luck haven't yet thickened her figure or etched the permanent scowl lines into her face. She has no reason yet to envy Imogene, no prescience of Imogene's living comfortably out in Port Angeles with her own car and her own house and enough left over from her paychecks to buy extravagant presents for Doris's own daughters, maybe even woo them away from her. What Doris sees in late 1936 is Imogene drudging away at that distant school near Winnett while Lud, back in Denton, looks for any way he can to scrape up a dollar. No future for those two, not for a long time. So why Doris's antagonism?

Friday, November 13, 1936. Letter from Lud—good news about horses . . .

Wednesday, December 2, 1936. Letter from Lud. Promised me a box of candy. . . .

Wednesday, December 9, 1936. Letter from Dad & two from Lud. Poor kid. Spending his money to fix that old wreck of a car & for what?

Thursday, December 10, 1936. Gee, I'm blue. . . .

Wednesday, February 10, 1937. Letter from Lud. He seems very blue. . . .

Tuesday, February 16, 1937. And the days go by———

"And that's *all?*"
"Of course, she had Aunt Mable's life for a pattern."

What kind of an ending would we write for Imogene if we could? Do we want to see her married and stuck on some godforsaken ridge or coulee ranch in Fergus County, spending her days scrubbing and baking and helping with the harvest and the cattle? Holding together a few depleted acres? Or not even that much—having to work for wages on somebody else's acres? For the sake of Lud's dark face and his grin and the tension in his arms? Imogene? Without resources, without choices? What kind of a story would that be?

On the other hand, why did she have to go to Port Angeles and live alone for the rest of her days? Why the harshness of her alternatives?

Imogene's diary entries continue through 1937, through another spring of worrying about her "apps" for next year's school, wherever it might be, through the tedious chores and the lists of the books she is reading, the letters she gets from home, the occasional personal reflection.

> *Sunday, April 4, 1937. A year ago Doris was married. . . .*

By late May she has applied to a dude ranch for summer work and been turned down, but she has heard from her father, who is working as a watchman at the Fort Peck dam project, that he thinks he can get her a summer job. She sees Lud briefly before she leaves:

> *Saturday, May 29, 1937. Lud came early—we left after lunch,*
> *I got my hair done in Lewistown. We went to the Deerfield dance.*

What follows is one of the most painfully boring summers ever recorded. Imogene finds herself stranded in Fort Peck with nothing to do—apparently the job, like so many of her father's assurances, came to nothing—*of course he wasn't fixed for us*—in suffocating northern-Montana heat, without other resources, so Imogene and her mother sit and crochet potholders, day after day, week after week. Her desperation resounds in every line of her stark entries:

> *Sunday, June 20. Meat loaf for dinner. O—for a job.*

> *Monday, June 21. Thundering hot day.*

> *Tuesday, June 22. Washed.*

> *Wednesday, June 23. Ironed—Read book. Remember the Day.*

> *Thursday, June 24. What a life.*

> *Friday, June 25. O—for a job—even part time work—anything to kill time.*

Only occasionally does introspection break in. *Hope I never put in such a summer but suppose I'll see the time when I will long for the leisure of these slow passing days,* she writes, and, a few days later, *Guess I'm an introvert. I live within myself—but of my most important thots & hopes & dreams I cannot even discuss with my mother. She still would like to see me finish college. If anything happens to Lud or our affair or plans I probably will but O for my own home—garden— cellar—chickens, pigs & milk cows—flowers—cattle.*

In July she hears that she has the Fairfield School for the coming year, but it's only forty dollars a month—and in August the Fairfield School board asks her to resign her contract because they want to consolidate with another district. She refuses, she has no other job in sight. Lud hauls her belongings to the Fairfield teacherage for her, and they go to a show and go roller-skating.

Then very little about Lud for a long time. Her diary entries have to do with the school and the people she meets in Fairfield.

She sounds much less depressed and lonely here than she did in Roy or Winnett. And yet—

Sunday, October 31. Lud came—took me to town—Sunday school—home for dinner & then goodbye—wonder when we'll meet again.

And on January 1, 1938, the entry that seems ominous in retrospect—*Makes me sick to think of my Hope Chest trunk being stolen.*

Her entries for the rest of that school year seem innocuous enough. The school-board elections, the neighborhood gossip, her teaching and her usual worries about a job for next year. Her sister Sylva invites her to stay with her and her husband in Washington State next summer. She accepts a date from a fellow and then wishes that she hadn't, he seems so fresh. Lud is notable only because she never mentions him. But not until April 4 do we know what has been brewing, and even then not what she had sensed of it— perhaps nothing.

Monday, April 4, 1938. Letter from Lud saying today he & Lewis go to Deer Lodge over a saddle. So I guess we are washed up. It gave me a jolt. He wrote April 1, I hadn't heard a thing. Doris didn't mention it.

Deer Lodge. The Montana State Penitentiary.

"What happened?" says Elizabeth.

I know what happened, though not why it happened, because I

have the article from the Lewistown *Democrat-News* for Saturday, March 26, 1938:

TWO ARRESTED
AND HELD ON BURGLARY

PICKED UP IN ROY SECTION ON A
SADDLE STEALING CHARGE

Ludwig Lind and Lewis Martinec of the Roy section are being held in the county jail on a charge of burglary. They were arrested Friday by members of Sheriff Tullock's force on a complaint brought in justice court by County Attorney J. E. McKenna charging them with the burglarizing of a building belonging to Richard Komarek residing a few miles northeast of Roy and the theft of a saddle from the building sometime Thursday night or Friday morning.

A few days later:

2 SENTENCED
PENITENTIARY SADDLE THEFT

LEWIS MARTINEC AND LUDWIG LIND
GIVEN MINIMUM OF ONE YEAR EACH
UPON ENTERING GUILTY PLEAS

Lewis Martinec, 24 of Roy and Ludwig Lind, 25 of Denton who waived their statutory rights and entered pleas of guilty when arraigned before Judge Stewart McConochie in district court Wednesday on a saddle stealing charge, were both sentenced to serve one year in the state penitentiary at Deer Lodge. . . . Taking into consideration the fact that this was the first legal offense either had been officially charged with and that they both plead guilty to the charge as entered, Judge McConochie in pronouncing sentence stated that he would reduce the penalty to the minimum.

So that's the whole sorry story, Elizabeth. Imogene was right. She and Lud were washed up. She was not a woman from the family or background that could have seen his arrest and sentencing as anything but disgrace for him and absolute humiliation for herself.

11

/ / /

Although Kay has warned me that eventually it
would happen, I am unprepared for the afternoon I go to visit my
aunt and she does not recognize me. She has shrunk down to
eighty-seven pounds by now, and her eyes swim out of her skull
to search my face and search past me. I know that Kay has changed
her antidepressant medication to Prozac to try to stem her tears.
What are the side effects of Prozac, what are the side effects of
the drugs she is given to control her high blood pressure, to reg-
ulate her blood sugar, to prevent goiter, to reduce the risk of
blood clots, to prevent seizures?

I read about people who have taught themselves to analyze and
question their prescriptions, but I have stopped trying to keep
track. I feel overwhelmed by the weight of the load. Separately,
every medication is working. My aunt's blood pressure, her blood
sugar are within acceptable levels. She's only eighty-one. Her

mother lived to be ninety-six. Aunt Mable lived to be eighty-eight. So every month I receive a three-page itemized printout from the pharmaceutical company in Salt Lake City that supplies the Villa Villekula, and I write a check on my aunt's account for the three or four hundred dollars at the bottom of the last page.

Meanwhile my aunt is restless, she cannot sit still in a chair long enough to hear a letter read to her, but she must be up and pacing the linoleum corridors—back and forth, back and forth all day, the aides tell me. She has worn through the soles of her shoes. What drives her? Is it the drugs, or the combination of the drugs? Or, as an elderly friend warns me, is her restlessness another predictable stage in her disintegration? I don't know. I am past anger, past worry, down to the bone. After a fifteen-minute visit with my aunt, I flee back to my office and, when the English-department secretary glances up from her word processor and says, "Are you all right?" I break down in tears.

That night in Boise, when a friend said, "Hello from Pete Daniels," my blood seemed to stop, and he looked at me curiously.

"Pete Daniels; yes, it's been years, I should write to him," I heard myself answer, and then knew what I wanted to do. Late that same night, emboldened by the wine I had drunk with dinner, I went up to my room and thought about the young woman I had been and wrote a note to the boy, no longer a boy, now a stranger, whom I had loved twenty years ago.

So you were in Idaho last week. How strange to think of your being so close—not thirty miles. No wonder I've been dreaming about you. I hope all is well with you, and that all the old wounds healed.

I stamped the envelope and mailed it from the hotel lobby and told myself that that was that. When a letter came back a week later, with its typewritten address, with the return address of a great southwestern university, I carried it in from the mailbox and dropped it on my desk until I was able to open it and read the polite typed words.

What did I expect? I keep asking myself. What did I hope for? The only answer I can come up with is that at least my past won't have ghosts.

And yet I keep the letter and read and reread it, deconstructing the lines for every possible nuance:

> *My wounds, real and imagined, are in pretty good shape, I think. I still smolder on some accounts, but even those seem to have become more of a resource than a liability. What a long strange trip it's been. . . . I hope you will keep in touch, and don't let 20 years elapse this time.*

Then the part that keeps me rereading, the postscript in the familiar handwriting. *Interpret your dreams for me . . . that's amazing.*

Imogene's shame stands out in the few lines she writes about Lud's arrest and sentencing:

Saturday, April 9, 1938. Cleaned house & ironed. Letter from Ma. She had just heard about Lud—took it like a brick. However could he do it.

And that is all for a long time.

Sunday, May 1, 1938. Sylvia is 30 today. Such a dreary day, & lonesome—no company . . . Nora brot my milk—cat had kittens. . . .

The teacherage is a single room behind the school. Imogene cooks a meal of bacon and fried potatoes on the coal stove and eats it by herself. No company today, nobody venturing out under a lowering sky that withholds all but a spat of sharp rain against the windowpane. The schoolyard gate stays shut, the bunchgrass grows undisturbed between the ruts of the road.

Gradually the gray light darkens, and she lights the lamp, glad to see the passing of Sunday, dreading Monday. Will she sleep tonight? What if she can't sleep? Her thoughts skitter around the edge of the abyss. She feels the onset, the falling apart, the imminent disintegration of her self into infinite fragments *lost whirling in the lamp flame what if she starts to cry again and can't stop with no one to hear will she still exist what to do to stop this when she can't breathe wants to scream can't escape has got to stop this.*

She has got to stop this. She is all alone out here, miles from town, and in any case there is nobody in the world to whom she would dare to speak of the abyss. Finally she gives up on sleep. Props pillows between herself and the iron headboard of the double bed and turns up the wick on the lamp and fits her embroidery hoop on a new pillowcase. She has to tilt the hoop to the light to see the stamped pattern of a lady with a bell skirt worked in dozens of tiny lazy daisy stitches.

She splits her floss, threads her needle with purple, anchors it with a knot, and casts the first of the lazy daisies. Oh, better. The soft rasp of thread through fabric soothes her. The easy repetitious pattern spins an illusion between her and the abyss. Better, better. She casts and stabs, casts and stabs, creating her own fragile comfort in thread.

Ever wonder why the women crocheted all those lace doilies and starched and ironed them and pinned them like so many white cobwebs over every piece of furniture? Ever wonder why all the embroidered pillowcases? All the embroidered dishtowels? All the embroidered dresser scarves with the crocheted edges lining the rooms with the bare studs of walls and the rusty linoleums and the windows that looked out at pointless horizons? If they looked long enough into the windows, they could see their own faces reflected back at them, and the terrors that they had to keep secret.

I never knew she was unhappy, said my mother. *I never knew.*

And yet Imogene has not let go, not entirely.

Monday, May 16, 1938. Letters from Ma & Lud—pictures.

So he wrote to her from prison. Did she add his letters to the bundle she left in the attic of the homestead shack, and did she write back to him?

/ / /

What would Lud have told Imogene about his experiences during the six months that he served of his sentence in the Montana State Penitentiary?

The prison in 1938 was probably not much changed from 1931, when a legislative committee saw inmates *lying idle, rotting away in stink and stench. The place as it is, is lousy with bed bugs and the cells are dark and grimy.* The effects of the Depression had permeated Montana's state government, and especially its penitentiary, where corrupt or inept administrators had kept even the sorry trickle of funds from improving a cellblock built in 1896. *Two buckets sufficed in each cell; one for drinking and the other for human waste. . . . A woefully inadequate electrical wiring system barely supported in each cell a single twenty-five watt bulb, too dim to read by,* writes a contemporary historian. The 1931 legislative committee described the old cellblock *as crying out in its filth,* and the isolation area beneath the ground floor of the new cellblock as *a hideous place to throw a man.*

The young man probably thought he was tough, probably even thought he knew a lot. Imogene, whose life had been relatively sheltered, might cry, *However could he do it,* but he might have answered her with *Easy. That's how.*

Needs must. None of Lud's plans was working out. Horsebreaking, rodeoing? No quick money there, no matter what his dreams told him. And a dollar a day was what he could earn at ranch work, supposing there was work to be had, during haying season or harvest season. What did he have to look forward to, what of his lot could he ever expect to improve? He would have known Imogene was losing heart.

And what about Imogene's young brother-in-law, Jack Hogeland, who also was breaking horses during those very years, though seldom for cash? Nobody had much money. Jack was breaking horses to harness for the use of them, for the harrowing and seeding and cutting of scant crops on land which at least was his own. Disappointment spurred the back-biting between the sisters, the spiteful words behind each other's backs, the doubts that Imogene had to swallow during those long afternoons and nights alone in her teacherage:

> *What does Lud know about breaking horses, compared with Jack?*
> *At least Jack's got his own ranch.*
> *Lud will never amount to anything. No more than Pa did. Ma*
> *says to be thankful I have a job. Oh God will I have another job*
> *next September?*

And then the theft of the saddle—a neighbor's saddle, worth perhaps fifty dollars, or twenty-five dollars, or even less—which for Imogene was the ultimate humiliation of knowing her man had broken not just her rigid familial injunctions but also the settlers' code of trust between neighbors, but which for Lud may have been an act of assertion over his own, more elemental humiliation.

Whatever he may have written to Imogene, whatever bravado he may have been able to disguise himself with, his six months in the Montana State Penitentiary taught Lud one thing: the enormity of what he was really up against.

After the Fairfield School ended its year in May of 1938, Imogene came back to Fergus County and lived on the ranch with her mother and father for the rest of the spring and the summer. Doris and Jack were living on the old Barney ranch, less than a mile for her to walk or ride down through the bluffs to the Judith River, and she visited them more and more often, beginning that emotional shift that would see her drawing closer and closer to her younger sister's family. Many of her diary references now are to horses or events that I can remember being told about. Others are mystifying, tantalizing, indecipherable.

Friday, June 10, 1938. Rained a little—not enuf to get wash water—to much to clean the attic—Doris came & brot us meat. Malvin & Bud came about Dolly.

Saturday, June 11, 1938. Ma & I prospected for a well. Jack & Joe came for the walking plow to ditch with.

Sunday, June 12, 1938. Malvin & Bud brot Dolly home with my saddle. Doris & Jack came for a while & I went home with them to go to town tomorrow.

Monday, June 13, 1938. Saw the sheriff. . . . Now what— Hope to get Myrtle to do a little detective work.

Thursday, June 30, 1938. More quilting—not much else. Got favorable return on my writing test. Letter from Lud.

Malvin and Bud are Lud's brothers. It sounds as though they came and borrowed the mare, Dolly, that Lud had given to Imogene, for the weekend. What about her saddle? Had they borrowed it, too, or had Lud had it? I have no way of knowing, although I remember the saddle clearly; it hung in our barn for years. It was one of those old-fashioned bronc saddles with high swells and a high cantle, and it had the soft, frayed patina of leather that has been used for a long time. It must have been at least as valuable as the saddle Lud served six months for, and it would bring an absurd price as antique tack today.

Joe is my father's teen-aged cousin, Joe Murray, who, until he enlisted in the navy in 1942, lived with my parents on the ranch during the summers. After the war Joe came back to work for my father, and I think it may have been Imogene's saddle that he used to ride. Maybe she gave it to Joe, she always liked him. One more of her possessions that she had to leave behind when she left Montana, one more scrap to gather dust and finally vanish.

Myrtle may be the cousin of my father's who still lives on the ranch at Sample's Crossing, on the Judith River. It is her husband, Noisy, whose photograph hangs in the Cowboy Hall of Fame. I don't know what sort of detective work Myrtle might have been asked to do, or why Imogene went to see the sheriff, who in 1938 was the same Mr. Guy Tullock whose deputies had arrested Lud.

"I met Guy Tullock once," Imogene told me years ago. "I went to see him about my hope chest that was stolen. He wouldn't do anything."

A jettisoned saddle, jettisoned hopes. First the tangibles, then the memories. Maybe Imogene's visit to the sheriff was her way of facing one more of her illusions as a loss and writing it off.

Imogene spent the rest of the summer of 1938 riding horseback and helping Doris and Jack with ranch work.

Sunday, July 3, 1938. I rode the south fence—Jack, Joe, & Doris came—looked & looked for the horses. . . . Got the colts branded at last.

Monday, July 4, 1938. Last night we started to the rodeo— broke an axel—borrowed Noisy's car—& had to walk home.

Wednesday, July 6, 1938. We chased Dolly for 2 hours & all got mad. Ran Pet down. Spilled half my water getting home. Rode from 3:30 till 9:00.

Thursday, July 7, 1938. Rode with Doris about 50 miles looking for horses. We got home about 10:00 P.M. Didn't find the horses but got track of them. Dolly got sore footed.

The ride Doris and Imogene made on July 7 of 1938 was their famous one. My father used to shake his head—"And when they told me how far they'd rode, and where they'd been, I just couldn't hardly *believe*—"

"We were looking for the horses. We just kept riding a little farther, just over another hill," my mother sniffed. "We didn't think anything about it."

The part of the story that Imogene told me was how their mother had fretted over Doris: "A young married woman shouldn't ride that far. She *might* be pregnant."

"And I knew one young married woman who *was* pregnant," Imogene always added, "but I was keeping quiet about it."

But in July of 1938? When I wasn't born until December of 1939?

Another of the family legends at odds with the facts.

But at least can we count on the permanence of landscape? Where Doris and Imogene rode that day was around the base of the South Moccasin Mountains, almost all the way to the tiny community of Hanover and back again. Doris was riding Pardner, my father's top horse, and Imogene was riding Dolly. Clouds would have rolled over the low blue peaks into a dry July sky and passed in shadows over the bunchgrass, and the sun bore down heavily until, approaching the long Montana twilight, it reddened and sank. Perhaps, as the sky darkened and purpled, a dry lightning storm moved across the benchland on the other side of the Judith River. The young women could see the landmarks they had known all their lives. The glint of the grain elevators at Danvers and at Ware, miles away in the weird light, and the scaffolding of the railroad bridge, miniaturized by distance, that stretched across the throat of the river gorge. Wind riffled the buckbrush in the coulees and flattened the bunchgrass and tore at the clumps of paintbrush and the heads of the balsamroot. Sweat had dried white on the flanks of the horses.

Somewhere the women spotted tracks, and somewhere they decided to turn back. If they were rained or hailed on, they joked, they were a long way from shelter. But they were Montana-born and unworried, and they rode easily on their unshod horses and talked—about what?

Not about her letters from Lud, if Imogene knows what is good for her. Not a word will she speak to her sister about her deepest feelings. Anyway, something is happening to her feelings. As they grow inward, they grow blunted. Numb. She shrugs to herself. *Just the way things are.* It's almost completely night now. Doris is a shape riding along the other rut of the road, silent with fatigue. Darkness leaches meaning from the landscape. The women have lost direction. Coulees and cutbanks gape out of the shadows, sagebrush sends up a quickening scent as the air cools. Where is the turnoff, where is the gate? But the horses know their way home. Tired, they quicken their pace. Sore-footed, Dolly stumbles once.

Imogene sends out her job applications, and on August 1 she hears that she has the Hilger School for the coming year. This is good news. Hilger is only a few miles from Lewistown. It has a store and a post office, and its school has two rooms, primary and secondary. Imogene will be teaching the four primary grades at eighty-five dollars a month. In September her diary resumes its familiar chronicle of repetitive days at school, small tasks, the pleasure of letters from home.

> *Monday, October 3, 1938. I started Oliver Twist. Wonder if Lud really gets out today. I hate to see him yet want to get it over.*

> *Saturday, October 15, 1938. I had a letter from Lud, who is working on a ranch.*

> *Saturday, November 19, 1938. Did very little shopping. . . . Think I saw Lud at a distance. Ma has seen him.*

> *Thursday, November 24, 1938. Lud stopped to ask Jack if he'd seen his horse—told me I'd get my $50 back. Went back with Doris & Jack.*

And so, in desperation, trying to replenish her sense of her self, Imogene turns to her younger sister, to the very sister who judges her.

> *Agree with Doris. Accept her judgment. At least it's a way of understanding, it's a way of telling the story that makes sense. Lud borrowed fifty dollars from me? And he's never paid it back? Just goes to show that he's been a skunk all along.*

So Imogene goes down to the Barney ranch almost every weekend to see Doris and Jack. To be sure of her welcome, she lends her car, lends money. Does ranch chores, helps out after the baby is born, takes care of little Mary, and gradually lets herself slip into a role on the fringe as Auntie. Of course she dates occasionally, she's only twenty-nine. But she can't stand it when a man tries to touch her, tries to kiss her. She is in abeyance. No feelings at all, perhaps. Except when she catches sight of the hulking dark figure at the other end of the street, the angle of his head and his big shoulders as familiar as the tips of her own fingers, the line of his back as he walks away. She feels sick. *How could he—how can she—*

She would die if anyone knew.

Then nausea stabs her. The pit widens under her feet—*Here it comes again, she is falling apart*—she has to rush at her schoolwork, play with the baby, wait until night, when she can scribble the one or two lines she allows herself. Finally the ink scrawl absorbs her terror, and she can sleep.

The fear of being alone—the fear of annihilation. I know more about the night terrors than I want to tell. And I know other women who skirt the edges, who prefer to keep their dread a secret. If loss of feeling is the alternative to the agony of abandonment, who can blame us?

In March of 1992, in an attempt to give the endangered wild-salmon hatchlings a chance to survive the long swim from their spawning beds to the Pacific Ocean through the turbines and bypass tunnels of the eight major hydroelectric dams on the Snake and Columbia rivers, the governor of Idaho ordered the Snake to be drawn down to its original level of eighteen years ago, before the construction of the dams had deepened and widened its flow. Conservationists hoped that the lower river level and the swifter current would help the salmon hatchlings endure the trauma of the long swim and the passage through the tunnels to the ocean with enough strength left to survive to adulthood and eventually return to spawn in their own beds.

A futile attempt, others were calling the Snake River drawdown. The salmon were already too few. Hacked to pieces by the generators, too heavily fished, too close to extinction to save. A recovery team estimated that a thousand returning adults would be needed every year for eight years before the wild sockeye salmon could be taken off the endangered-species list; in 1992 only one returning male sockeye would be tallied at the spawning beds in Idaho's Stanley Basin on the Snake River.

For months the lobbies and the economic-interest groups battered Governor Andrus with letters and threats of lawsuits, trying to get him to rescind the draw-down order. What about irrigation water? What about damage to the marinas? What about recreational water for boating, for water skiing, for touring? When nobody even knows if the salmon can be saved? But Governor Andrus resisted these pressures, and what followed was a draw-down process which I and everybody else living at the confluence of the Snake and the Clearwater watched with fascination as the great river shrank by inches before our eyes.

On mornings when I drove Rachel to school along Snake River Avenue, she and I looked to see what had happened to the river while we slept, and in the mild spring evenings we walked out on the levee and marveled at how far the support pillars of the bridges had risen out of the water. The Lewiston *Morning Tribune* ran feature articles about a re-emerging landscape of inlets and eddies that no one had seen in eighteen years, and the widening wet stretches of mud on both sides of the river drew children as though

they were returning to primordial slime. The fire department had
to throw ropes and drag out one young man who ventured too
far and sank to his waist in mud.

But, as the river gave up its secrets—a car that had been driven
into the current for reasons best known at the time, a crashed
airplane, the thousand-year-old sites of villages and burial grounds
mentioned in the Lewis and Clark journals, the partial skeleton
of a man gone missing from the Nez Percé reservation a few
years ago—I found myself increasingly preoccupied with the re-
emergence of the river itself. For five years I had been driving to
work and home again along that broad platinum flow, so still and
so deep that it barely seemed liquid. I had seen its colors shifting
with the light, its surface convoluted into indecipherable patterns
by the speedboats or beaten into gold shingles by the evening wind.
Now I saw that, beneath that molten surface, buried under those
tons of slowly moving water, a tough western river with real
gravel bars and a real current had been flowing all along.

Soon they'll let the reservoirs fill up again, and the river will rise, I
wrote to a friend. *Apparently it's not possible to have the placid surface
and the mean current at the same time.*

The phone is ringing. I struggle up from sleep. The digital clock
by my bed says 2:00 A.M. Still too dazed to feel alarm—*Has Auntie
died?*—I fumble for the receiver and say, "Hello?"

A pause.

"Hello, this is Pete Daniels," he says from a thousand miles
away.

/ / /

Teaching in Hilger in the fall of 1938, Imogene starts a creative-writing course by correspondence. She daydreams about earning money from her writing, supplementing her salary—she cannot save or get ahead on eighty-five dollars a month. Her roommate, Ruth, begins a hot romance with a man named Chet, to Imogene's disgust—she can hear them on the couch at night after she has gone to bed. The winter drags on, finally passes. Imogene tries valiantly to lose weight, starves down to a hundred and fifty pounds. She is courted by an older man who irritates her.

Friday, March 24, 1939. Mr. B asked to see me home. Ick.

Then comes another puzzling sequence of entries.

Monday, March 27, 1939. Had a letter from Dave & one from Lud—who said Dolly was still mine & he would bring her back to me.

Thursday, April 13, 1939. Had a good letter from Doris. She said Lud was down & let on he had not had Dolly. I sent her his letter. He told me he had her.

Saturday, May 13, 1939. Got a letter from Doris. She made me blue. I was blue all day.

Friday, May 26, 1939. Ma & I sewed & cleaned & talked. In the evening we took a walk up on the hill & saw a rider & lead horse go down the canyon. I'm in hopes it was Lud & that I will get Dolly.

Just what was going on between Lud and Imogene over the mare Dolly can only be conjectured. Dolly had gone sore-footed after the fifty-mile ride in July of 1938, and Imogene turned her out to pasture and rode a mare named Beauty for the rest of that summer. Occasionally during the fall she will note, *Saw the horses,* and in late December she writes, *I rode over to the ranch for a book. Did not see the other horses.* But if Dolly was missing by the end of December, and if Imogene and Doris were speculating on what might have become of her, the diary doesn't tell.

It could be that Lud needed a horse, and so on one overcast afternoon he slipped up to Jack's winter pasture on the slope of the South Moccasins, where Dolly was running with the rest of the horses, and he roped her out of the bunch and rode her for the rest of the winter and into the spring of 1939. Dolly was gentle and willing and useful, by all accounts. And it could be that Lud thought of Dolly as his, in a way. She had been his once; he had given her to Imogene years ago. Or it could be that he thought he was getting away with something. Dolly would have been worth a little money.

Or is it possible that Dolly had become the last tangible link that held Lud and Imogene together, a link that neither wanted to let go?

Imogene ends the sequence with a terse and baffling narrative:

Saturday, May 27, 1939. Ma went to Kingsbury's for the mail & while she was gone Lud came. He rode Dolly & led a black he said he'd ridden, but not alone or out of a corral. Gee I was sick with worry. I think he got knocked out by the well. At least he went to Kingsburys to get one to haze. . . .

And then the outburst.

Sunday, May 28, 1939. Doris came up for a while. Ma & I did not get much done. . . . Lud came this afternoon with Dolly. What the rest say about him makes no difference to me. He can't lie or steal faster than those who have never been caught.

And that's it, Elizabeth. That's all.

In late May of 1992 the Seattle-Tacoma International Airport is undergoing renovation, and I walk through dusty plywood-lined corridors with my shoulder bag and my book bag, wondering what I think I am doing. When I reach the Alaska Airlines gates I drop my bags on one of the plastic seats to wait for my connecting flight to the Southwest. This end of the terminal is jammed with people waiting for flights to Ketchikan and Anchorage and Fairbanks, and it occurs to me that perhaps that is the direction I should take.

Mary, you didn't—*tell us you didn't*—no, you wouldn't dream of rearranging your class schedule and buying a plane ticket and taking your aging face and body off to visit a man you haven't seen in twenty years?

Earlier in the spring, Brian had been restless. He and Elizabeth had been married, and he had settled into a fall and winter of cooking, taking care of the baby, working, and playing gigs on weekends to pay the bills and keep the household running while Elizabeth studied. Now he had a night off, and all he wanted was to go down to the Alibi Bar and listen to a band. Not just any band, but a group up from Boise that he used to play steel guitar with. He wanted to have a few drinks and visit with the guys on their break and remember the days when he had been a serious musician.

Would Elizabeth go with him? No, she would not. She had to study. Her immunology final was on Monday, and then came her epidemiology final, and her pathology final—

"Call Mother," she suggested. "See if she'll go with you."

Your *mother* and your *husband* went out drinking together? exclaim Elizabeth's friends the next day, all aghast.

But it strikes Brian and me as a wonderful idea. I'm restless, too, I'm tired of staying home and working on a Saturday night, and if I'm reduced to going out with my son-in-law, so be it.

I get Rachel settled, and then I head up to Brian's, where he is putting the baby to bed. Brian pours me a whiskey and finishes diapering the baby and puts his pajamas on him, and then he pours himself a whiskey and joins me at the kitchen table, where we wait to make sure the baby goes to sleep so Elizabeth won't be disturbed. We're feeling good, we're looking forward to the evening. My classes are winding down, my academic year is almost over, and I'm ready for the Alibi. God, what a long time since I went honky-tonking! Brian puts on an old Nanci Griffith tape I haven't heard, and when it comes to her rendition of "Gulf Coast Highway" we sing along.

We don't realize how noisy we are until Elizabeth stalks out of the bedroom and gets herself a drink of water. She glares at us, she's ready to kill us for the racket we're making. Later she says that she thought, *Will they never leave?* and then, *Why am I staying home and studying while they have fun?*

But Brian and I are too relaxed to worry about Elizabeth's disapproval. We float out to my car and head downtown. It's early evening, the streetlights on Main Street are just glowing through the new foliage, and the air is as mild and soft as though, somehow, the earth still stands a chance and so do we. We're playing more Nanci Griffith in the car as we cruise the length of Main Street, turn in to the parking lot behind the Alibi, and spot an empty slot just as the driver of the Dodge Daytona ahead of us spots it, too, throws his gears into reverse, and slams right into my front bumper.

Brian leaps out to confront the moose who is getting out of the Daytona. When they start to circle each other, stiff-legged, I rush up with placating words, and so does the moose's girlfriend.

"Goddamn!" yells Brian. "Here I am, out with my mother-in-law for the evening, and you have to go and run into us!"

The moose looks perplexed. "Hell," he says, "how was I supposed to know she was your mother-in-law?"

As an apologia, this for some reason strikes me as enormously funny, and I can't stop laughing even as I inspect the damage to the front of my car, wring the name of his insurance carrier out of the moose, and tell Brian we may as well make the most of our night out. Laughter carries me into the Alibi, laughter buoys me over the slapping chords of country-western guitars, as high as the swirls of cigarette smoke rising above the palisades of empty beer bottles on ill-lit tables. Brian and I dance, and we drink beer, and we start laughing all over again—*How was I supposed to know she was your mother-in-law?* as though, had he but known, he never would have run into us—and we visit with Brian's friends in the band when they take their break. Toward closing time, when Brian goes to settle our tab, I sit laughing by myself, which seems to tickle a passing kid in a big hat and cowboy boots, because he stops and asks me to dance.

I'm laughing all the way home. One of those moments that fixes itself in memory: driving home under the shadows of the old rock terraces on Eighth Street, and then the winking traffic lights and the reflections on the water along Snake River Avenue. I think Brian is drunk. When I turn in to his driveway, I assess him again—yes, pretty drunk. A good chance he'll never remember what we talked about tonight. And so, for the first time, I speak what has been on my mind all evening, all spring.

"I've been thinking of going to see an old friend, but I've been afraid to tell Elizabeth about him."

Brian considers weightily.

"What would you think, Brian, if I did that?"

Never mind what Brian thinks, what do I think?

Twenty years ago Pete Daniels would not leave his wife for me. What reason do I have to think that he wants me now? The real man is not, after all, a projection of my imagination with a name borrowed from local legend. I know Pete Daniels will never bring me balsamroot. And yet I could wish for his control over narrative, for some of the self-igniting charge of dynamite that he has used to blast his life out of the predictable. Pete Daniels with a Ph.D. in English?

"I think you ought to go for it," says Brian after a long silence.

12

/ / /

Elizabeth and I ride along the rim of the bare hill that looms above the Snake River. Leftover rain clouds roll off to the south, purpling the outcroppings of volcanic rock, but the late sun has broken out to streak the deep grass of Idaho. If I were to look back, I would see the rooftops of Lewiston and Clarkston far below us, and the green foliage of trees on both sides of the confluence of slow rivers, the Snake and the Clearwater, and their bridges remote and small, and the distant curls of smoke rising over the pulp mill like an unreadable message in the gray haze. But I don't look back. Up here is sky and dry weeds, a good trail, and sensations I thought I had forgotten.

The mares have been ridden too little this spring, and they dance and spook at pheasants and badger holes and trash, for we are never out of the sound of traffic up here, never out of sight of the housing developments. And yet I can imagine how we must look from far below, from one of those new subdivision decks, perhaps, if one happened to glance up and spot those ospreys wheeling in the wind currents above the rocks and then, far away, the two women on horseback, sun glinting on the tails of the sorrel and the bay just before they disappear into the tawny grass, like a last glimpse before a page is turned.

Not a trail I ever thought I'd ride. Not here in Idaho, where the light falls in sharp edges and the irrevocable crags and bare grass plummet seven hundred feet down to the Snake. Certainly not here on the margins of town. But, God, it feels good to be on horseback again. My mare isn't young, but she dances sideways, and I've still got my balance, I still know how to ride. In my father's saddle, with a good horse under me, I feel the fragmented parts of my life are settling together.

"You post?" I ask Elizabeth when she rides up beside me at a hard trot.

"Yes, always," she says, surprised, "it's how I learned."

I never knew anybody to post in the old days. They say it's easier to post, but I can ride forever the way my father rode, with a cowboy's flat seat. The years of riding my father's saddle with his stirrups too long for me got me in the habit; I still ride with my legs nearly straight, and I lean back into my father's silhouette.

Why give up riding for years? Was it because I thought I could be his daughter or my own woman but not both?

"I never could please him," Elizabeth says. "Never, no matter how hard I rode."

He has been dead nearly ten years. How could he have imagined Elizabeth and me, his granddaughter and his daughter, a vet-med student and a professor of English, reconciled with each other after the hard years, riding Idaho on these aging mares he bred over in Montana? And yet what would he have imagined for us, what would he have wanted for us?

Hearts are not had as a gift, but hearts are earned—for years I would have disagreed with Yeats, believed that the only heart worth having was the heart that came as a gift.

When I was in my teens, I rode green colts for my father while he hazed for me on a gentle saddle horse. As we rode, he talked of horses and I listened. All the dead horses, a litany of names. Bess and Bauley, Socks and Babe. Pardner and Pet, who were old Midge's colts. Midge herself, and Banty and Juley—

I don't remember any of those horses, Elizabeth told me once.

But I remember them. The shapes of workhorses, gentle giants lumbering down the lane behind the barn. Massive shoulders, heavy fetlocks. Their ears pricked for the sounds of human voices. Socks and Babe, Star and Dixie, Bess and Bauley. Always in pairs, unable to separate even to graze after the years of pulling in double harness. The geldings in particular would get frantic and thrash and whinny if the mares were led out of sight.

In a black-and-white snapshot taken forty years ago, old Bess is tied up by the log shop, peaceable in the late-June sun. Memory animates the pose, extends it outside the beveled edge of the snapshot. Bess's tail occasionally flicks at a fly, but she does not otherwise shift as my father lifts her huge forefoot and braces it against his thigh to clean and trim her hoof. His little girls scramble to pick up and examine the curved slices of discarded hoof, which are limber and brittle at the same time, live matter and yet not alive.

"Don't get around behind her," he warns. "She might not see you and step on you."

He trims her mane and tail, dropping the long coarse black hairs in the dirt for us to gather and try to braid, although the hairs resist us, spring apart in our fingers. He is getting the horses ready for haying season, and he is particular about their appearance; his teams are always trimmed and shod and well matched for color and size. He walks quickly back from the anvil with the horseshoe on tongs, and part of the sound of summer is the sharp tap-tap of his hammer on horseshoe nails. Later he might boost one of us up on Bess's broad back for the lofty ride back to the corral, where Bauley anxiously whinnies for her.

My father must be in his middle thirties that June, supporting his mother and his wife and his two little girls on the ranch on Spring Creek. Somewhere in the back reaches of thought he strides about his work. He wears boots with undershot heels and Levi's washed to pale-blue velvet and a blue chambray shirt. He is thinking about his ripening hay, about his aging workhorses, about his white-faced calves fattening on the grass on the summer slopes. Hardly on his mind at all is the slow dissolve, the collapse of corrals and sheds and fences, the house jacked up on wheels and moved away, the ranch itself no longer a ranch at all but somebody else's acreage. Those two little girls squatting in the dirt to play with horsehair, can he suppose them grown up and gone away? Not if he can help it.

"He never talked to me about horses, not in all the summers I stayed at the ranch," Elizabeth tells me now. "Never but once. When the other kids teased me because my 4-H colt was so much smaller than the quarter horses they were riding, Grandpop told me I shouldn't feel bad, because the best horse he ever had was just as small as her, and a bay like her—"

"That was Midge."

She looks at me in surprise. "Yes, he said her name was Midge."

I can see that the name sounds no special reverberations for Elizabeth. But I try to explain to her what it sounds for me, and how I can just barely remember Midge as a shadow at the edge of my earliest consciousness; and then I wonder, can I really see that patient silhouette when I shut my eyes, the shape of the small bay mare waiting at the barbed-wire gate at the end of a lane that no longer exists on earth?

Midge was Hambletonian, Joe Murray told me, *and Pardner was her colt, and he showed the Hambletonian blood when he trotted. When I was fifteen, I used to ride Pardner bareback. I'd keep a tight rein in each hand and kick him into that hard trot and lean over so I could watch his hoofs. He had a twenty-two-inch overreach.*

Now I tell Elizabeth about the entry about Midge I came across in one of Imogene's diaries.

Wednesday, June 21, 1944. Rode home this morning. Saw old Midget & think she is dying—poor thing. When I spoke to her she followed me a few steps & then lay down.

A few days later Imogene wrote, *Saw two coyotes feeding on Midget.*

Elizabeth shudders.

/ / /

After Lud brought Dolly back to her, Imogene taught another year at the Hilger School. Then, in the fall of 1940, she took the Duck Creek School for eighty dollars a month and a room with electric lights. It was the school where my father had finished the eighth grade, and where I would attend the fourth through seventh grades, and it sat on a low hill on the edge of wheat fields on the road to Lewistown. Teaching at Duck Creek meant that Imogene could see more of her family, especially her sister Doris, who often stopped by the school on her way to town to visit or to drop off Mary for an afternoon.

Thanksgiving dinners with Doris and her family. Christmas dinners. The occasional dances or visits to some of the Hogeland connections. The work of the ranch, gardening and harvesting, canning and butchering, repetitive and without surprises, as one year faded into another. Imogene lent a hand, lent money. She depended on her brother-in-law Jack for small services, changing the oil in her car or charging its battery for her. An uneventful life, but a calm life. Perhaps even a life with the potential for contentment.

And yet—*Letter from Doris. She's got everything & I've got nothing. She's been married 4 yrs. today. I've had lots of grief & lonely times & boring months.*

At the crest of the rocks Elizabeth and I rein in and look back at the two great altered rivers spread out like a map in miniature below us. From this distance, in the late-afternoon light, the Snake and the Clearwater look unchangeable as they roll toward their confluence. But their appearance is a deception. I had read how, when General Howard ordered the nontreaty Nez Percés out of their homelands and onto the reservation in the spring of 1877, they had begged him to let them wait until summer, when the high waters of the Snake would have gone down and they could safely ford their cattle and their children and old people. Howard refused, and so Yellow Wolf and the other young men rode their horses out into the river and stretched rawhide ropes to draw the people across. It was one of the incidents that touched off the Nez Percé rebellion, the flight into Montana, the battles at the Big Hole and the Bear's Paw, and their final surrender. But I never was able to visualize that river crossing until I saw the Snake drawn down this spring.

Imogene only mentioned Lud two or three more times in fifty years of diaries—perhaps two or three times in her life. Once, while she was shopping in the old Power's department store in Lewistown, she happened to glance out the window and see Lud on the sidewalk. He walked past that window several times while Imogene watched, but she didn't think he saw her.

And once, years later, after she had moved to Washington but had come back to Montana for her summer visit, she noted that she went to the Fergus County Fair and saw Lud on the midway.

Imogene had long daydreamed about going out to Washington to teach. About making a new start for herself. But now, in a comfortable rut, one day following another, she may have felt disinclined to send out the "apps" to the Washington school districts that always sent back refusals. Why try, why not drift—maybe next year, maybe the year after next, she would stir herself and try again.

And then it was the summer of 1942. The boys had gone off

to war, and hay was being put up along the Judith River meadows with teams of horses. Imogene was helping out with the haying that summer, riding a mowing machine behind her brother-in-law's spooky sorrel colts. One moment all was predictable. The next moment—the flick of an ear, the buzz of an insect in the sweet wild grass, and then the wild career, spinning blue sky and clouds reversing for clover and seedheads and wagon tongue—the teeth of the sickle bar had sliced into the soft flesh of her ankle, all the way to the bone.

Memories of horses are like patches of film on high-speed reverse. I get no more than a glimpse of the dark mare waiting at the end of the lane with her head down. Her life outran mine, as have the others'. I see my father working cattle on Pardner. The old brown gelding's cow sense tells him which way the yearling heifer is going to dodge before she does it. He swaps ends to head her off, his long brown head and his long forelegs doubling back against the momentum of his hindquarters. How can a horse so ungainly be so quick?

The lives of horses run parallel to ours in a different dimension of time. The muzzles of horses lift from the water trough, turning and dripping, ears pricked toward a voice, hazel-flecked eyes watching the carrier of oats through a dazzle of sun in slow motion. Twenty-five of our years is a horse's lifetime. Perhaps that is why they seem so vulnerable.

For the next ten years after she had left Montana and moved to the Olympic Peninsula, Imogene's diaries recorded her desire to marry, her longing for what she saw as security. In the meantime she was working toward a security of her own: the peace and squalor of the house on the bluff above Morse Creek, overlooking the Strait of Juan de Fuca and the distant lights of Victoria, Canada. Here she must have felt safe, unbuffeted. But her diaries will never again hint at involvement with any man beyond the most casual of friendships. She will never speak of the emotional bludgeoning she experienced as a young woman, nor will her close-written lines over fifty years tell whether she ever rode Dolly again, or why Lud's name floated out of the vortex as her mind began its final downward spiral into senility.

Rijule raises her head and inhales the faint wind. She is the same mare that Elizabeth broke to ride as a 4-H colt when she was in high school, the mare that reminded my father of Midge. The black forelock blows back from her chiseled Arabian face as she absorbs some message beyond our comprehension, deeper than the rocks and grass and farther away than the pale wash of colors and the blue tips of the Wallowas. The sound of unshod hoofs, the undulation of painted flanks following a trail, the shadows.

All the long-ago horses. The chore horse I used to ride, who found my way home for me through clouds and pines and the indistinguishable black shapes of underbrush and shadows—give me a horse between my legs and I'm still that girl, looking for my way—

And I think about that secret river under the tons of slow-moving water below us. At least now I know that its current still flows.

"So what did you do in Arizona?" Elizabeth had asked without real interest when I walked into her kitchen Monday afternoon.

I had started to cry somewhere over Zion National Park on the flight home, was still crying when the land turned green and pine-edged in the Pacific Northwest and I changed planes in Seattle for the short hop back to Idaho. Now I was crying again. I felt too ravaged not to answer her.

"I went to see Pete Daniels."

Elizabeth is not often at a loss for words, but she is now. Her mouth falls open. Her astonishment makes me cry harder.

"I just supposed you went to a conference, or something," she says finally. And then she says, "Why didn't you tell me? *Why didn't you tell me?*"

But I can't answer yet, and she studies me, perplexed. After a while she says, "So, how does he look?"

Not so much changed after twenty years. The jut of his nose and cheekbones grows sharper as he ages. Narrow-hipped and slightly bowlegged in his Levi's, as he always was. His shoulders are like a buffalo's. He is still Pete Daniels.

and god the pleasure of his arms after all these years the pleasure I thought I'd never know again his mouth on mine don't let me go this time don't let me go I'm not going to let you go but we both know he's lying too many reasons why we'll say goodbye in the morning

"He has three grandchildren," I tell her.

Elizabeth absorbs the idea of Pete Daniels as a grandfather while I cry into my thirtieth Kleenex. Then she returns to her inexorable question. "Why didn't you tell me, Mother?"

"Because—" I am trying to find the words. "When I look at you, I also see the child. I can't separate you from the child."

Something has dawned in her face. "You thought I'd judge you," she says.

"Yes!"

And I'm a flood of tears now, I'm a wreck, but the fragments are settling together. Is this what I'm going to be able to salvage? Elizabeth and my being able to talk?

Why do hearts have to be earned? How do these two women come to be riding the hill above the Snake River, through weeds and bolt holes, on a trail that soon will be no trail at all? For a realtor's sign has already been hammered into the sidehill, advertising lots for sale and a telephone number in colors that have bleached like the thistles in the sun. I think of Yellow Wolf and the emptiness he saw here, and I know I am as transitory as he, a fleeting glimpse of a bay horse and a rider before the light fades.

Somewhere behind us, on the plateau of the Lewiston Orchards, warm in the late sun, are the concrete-block walls and modest parking lot of the Villa Villekula, and somewhere in a room Imogene sits on the edge of her bed and twists her hands and trembles as she waits for whatever approaches. She has no past. Her only context is the present.

But I remember the names of the horses she rode as a young woman, and the secrets she kept; and I think of her scribbling her few lines night after night into her diaries, recording her life in the fragments that would, in a strange time and a strange place, reassemble themselves for me. Here on the verges of town, riding over the ruts dug by four-wheelers, where the weeds hold a dangerous litter of condoms and plastics and broken glass, I am myself.

And I hold that thought as my daughter and I ride down from the rocks, picking a way through badger holes and beer cans in the cooling grass, home toward the confluence of rivers in the deepening Idaho twilight.